VISION MOMENTS

TruthQuest

VISION MOMENTS

CREATING LASTING TRUTHS IN THE LIVES OF YOUR STUDENTS

BO BOSHERS
AND
KEITH COTE

BROADMAN
& HOLMAN
PUBLISHERS

NASHVILLE, TENNESSEE

0-8054-2725-2

Published by Broadman & Holman Publishers,
Nashville, Tennessee

Dewey Decimal Classification: 259.24
Subject Heading: STUDENT MINISTRIES—ADMINISTRATION
CHURCH WORK WITH STUDENTS

1 2 3 4 5 6 7 8 9 10 08 07 06 05 04

This book is dedicated to
student ministry leaders around the world
who teach God's Word and cast vision
to junior and senior high school students,
encouraging and challenging them to do life in Jesus' name.

It is our prayer that the material in *Vision Moments* will
help you continue to teach God's Word and to cast a strong,
clear vision to reach and lead this generation
into full devotion to Christ.

CONTENTS

PREFACE

Today more than ever, I am convinced that this generation needs a genuine vision of God's power and authority. Students need powerful experiences that help them understand that God can change their lives and their friends' lives and change the world around them. Students need to know that God is bigger than anything they face and that he will always be there for them. As student ministry leaders, we are responsible to cast a compelling vision—a vision worth following. We need to teach God's Word in dynamic, experiential ways that move students to respond with commitment and devotion. Simply put, students need leaders, and leaders lead with vision.

Vision Moments is a tool to equip you, the student ministry leader, to teach God's truth and to cast vision about the adventure of becoming fully devoted followers of Christ. It is designed to help you *inspire* students to have a heart for God and each other, to *motivate* them to take ownership, to *encourage* them to deepen their compassion to reach others, and to *instill vision* in them to impact the world with God's love and grace.

Never underestimate the power of a compelling vision. Vision is what moves students from the bleachers to the spiritual playing field. In fact, a clearly articulated vision could make the difference between *having a youth group* in which students are complacent and have a "been-there" attitude and *leading a student ministry* in which students are motivated and passionate about serving God and building his kingdom.

My prayer is that *Vision Moments* will enable you to cast a life-changing vision God can use to build a prevailing student ministry that impacts your church, your community, and the world.

—*Bo Boshers*

This generation learns best through stories. Students want to hear biblical truths told in ways that are relevant to real life. That's what Jesus did. Jesus was a master storyteller. He presented biblical truths within stories that connected to real life and made a lasting impact. Just think of the stories like the sower, the vine and the branches, and the good Samaritan. These are examples of *vision moments.* Jesus' listeners could relate to these stories and were able to connect with God through them.

Vision moments are powerful! They offer inspiration, encouragement, and hope. And they can be used by God to make a lasting impact on young hearts and lives.

My prayer is that *Vision Moments* will provide you with the essential tools you need to begin building lasting vision in the hearts of your students.

—*Keith Cote*

ACKNOWLEDGMENTS

We are indebted to many people who made significant contributions to the development of *Vision Moments*. These include:

Mike Lueth, a gifted volunteer who assisted us in so many ways. Your fingerprints are on every page of this book. It is a privilege to serve with you and call you friend.

Christine Anderson, director of product development at the Willow Creek Association (WCA). Thank you for your servant attitude and your hard work to help us get this project in shape. We are grateful for your talents and your friendship.

Steve Keels, point leader for the *TruthQuest* product line. Thank you for your vision to publish resources to help this generation love and understand the Word of God. We're so grateful to be part of your dream.

Lynette Rubin, longtime assistant to Bo, for your organization and patience in taking so many voice mails and e-mails, and bringing them together on the pages of this book.

Brandy Ogata, Pat McAndrew, Jackie Rietsma, and Retha Theron, WCA Student Ministries staff and volunteers, for your servant attitudes and a willingness to help out whenever there was a need.

Willow Creek Association staff for your commitment to providing vision, training, and resources to church leaders around the world. It is a privilege to be on the same team with you.

Troy and Tricia Murphy, Bruce Smith, and Bill Connor, all key players on the gifted and creative student ministry teams we've worked with over the years. Thank you for so many vision-filled, exciting, and fulfilling years together.

Jay and MaryJo Mooncotch, Dean and Diane Scheulter, Mike and Joyce Lueth, Dave and Sharon Christensen, and Dave and Kara Zimmerman—all good friends. Thank you for your consistent encouragement, support, and prayers.

Broadman & Holman staff, especially Gary Terashita, for patience and encouragement during the development of this project.

Our families.

Bo Boshers: Special thanks to my wife and best friend Gloria and my three heroes: sons Brandon and Trevor and my daughter Tiffany. Thank you for your prayers, support, and for believing in me. I love you with all my heart.

Keith Cote: Special thanks to my wife Angela, my best friend and biggest supporter. Thanks for always being there for me. I love you more than words can say. To my children Samuel, Graham, Madelyn, and Camille: you bring joy to my heart, laughter to our home, and excitement as I anticipate how God will continue to use you to impact your world. Thanks for your prayers and encouragement. I love you!

HOW TO USE
THIS BOOK

Vision Moments includes proven lessons designed to teach God's truth in creative, interactive, and fun ways. Through hands-on, experience-based learning, junior and senior high students discover how they can apply biblical truths to their everyday lives. In the process they are motivated and challenged to become the difference-makers God wants them to be.

Vision moments can be especially effective to begin or end a teaching series. For example, if you are beginning a teaching series on evangelism, starting with a vision moment is an excellent way to motivate students to reach their lost friends for Christ—and keep them coming back for the rest of your series. Or, if you are concluding a series on grace, you could use a vision moment to help students remember this truth. For example, in "A Renewed Heart," students learn that God not only forgives sins; he also forgets them. It's a difficult concept to grasp, but when students watch a white balloon with their sins written on it sail away into the sky, they have an actual experience to help them understand and remember the truth of this amazing gift.

The activities for each vision moment are best suited for groups of five to thirty students. If your group is larger than thirty, the activities can be effectively used by breaking into subgroups and having additional leaders teach the vision moment concurrently. Each vision moment is designed to be completed in approximately forty-five minutes. Many vision moments also include an object students take home so they have a visual reminder of the biblical truth they've learned.

The book features seventeen vision moments divided into five parts. Each part focuses on a key value of a prevailing student ministry:

1. Spiritual Growth: *A Heart for God*
2. Community: *Caring for Each Other*
3. Commitment: *Developing Student Ownership*
4. Evangelism: *A Heart for Others*
5. Service: *Impacting the World*

Part Overviews and Assessments

Each of the five parts opens with an overview and an assessment. The overview summarizes the biblical theme and teaching objective of that section and lists every vision moment to give you a quick read on the contents of that part.

The assessment is designed to help you evaluate your current ministry challenges and direct you to the best vision moment to meet that challenge. Read through the overviews for each section and complete the assessments to determine where your students have the greatest need for renewed vision. Then look at your ministry year and decide when it would be most strategic to cast the vision and raise the value in the lives of your students.

Vision Moments

Each vision moment includes the following elements:

Purpose: Offers a one-line summary of the teaching objective.

Overview: Provides the big picture by highlighting the key teaching points and Scriptures on which the teaching is based.

Materials: Includes a bulleted list of all needed materials.

Preparation: Lists step-by-step instructions to help you prepare to teach effectively.

Teaching Outline: Guides you through every aspect of the moment by detailing action steps and content in narrative form (as you would actually say it). The teaching outline includes three kinds of material:

1. **Teach:** Text following "Teach" subheads provides the basic narrative for each teaching point. These sections are complete but also intentionally brief. Although each vision

moment can be taught as is, we encourage you to add your own insights and to personalize the material to make it most meaningful to your ministry.

2. **Action:** Text following "Action" subheads lists things you are to do to deliver the content, for example, asking a student to read a Scripture verse or interacting with a teaching prop. Also included are instructions for individual, partner, and small-group activities.

3. **Pray:** Text following "Pray" subheads suggests one or two key ideas to include in your own prayers.

Create an Environment
That Honors Authentic Commitments

Vision moments can be used by God to help students make an authentic commitment to change their lives to become more like Christ. They use creative, experiential teaching to engage students' minds and also to impact their hearts. To do this, every vision moment challenges students to decide if they are ready to make a public commitment based on biblical truth. Some students may not be ready to make a commitment. That's OK. The goal is for students to make *authentic decisions,* not to follow the group based on fear of being shamed or singled out. From the beginning, it's very important to create an environment that honors process and gives students freedom to be completely honest with where they are spiritually. Students should never be made to feel unspiritual or disobedient for deciding not to make a commitment during a vision moment. We want them to make real decisions, not pretend decisions. In a safe and accepting environment, students are more open to hearing and responding to God's truth in authentic ways.

Here are three ways you can make your group a safe place for students to make authentic commitments.

1. *Before the moment, acknowledge that we're all in different places spiritually.* It's important to know where your students are spiritually. These vision moments were designed with Christian students in mind. If you have non-Christians in your group, you need to be especially sensitive to their needs as well as to the needs of Christian

students. One way to do this is to start by saying something like, "You're going to hear truths today that will issue a challenge you may not be ready for. Some of you don't yet have a personal relationship with Christ. You still have questions. Today may bring more clarity or more questions. You need to know you shouldn't feel obligated to make any decision before you're ready. We're all here to ask questions and seek answers and to learn more about who God is.

"If you are a Christian, today's challenge is for you. But it's a challenge that calls for an individual response. You shouldn't feel pressure to make a commitment you're not ready for either. It's important to listen to the Holy Spirit and make an honest decision based on his leading."

2. *During the moment, encourage students to be authentic in their commitments.* At the point in the vision moment that calls for a public commitment or decision, remind students that they shouldn't feel obligated to make a decision they aren't ready for. If they have questions or need more time to process the commitment, affirm the sincere decision to wait. You might say something like, "In just a moment, you'll have an opportunity to make a commitment. Some of you may not feel ready to make this commitment—you have questions or you need more time. You need to know I respect your decision to be authentic about where you are. Others of you are ready to make this commitment. You need to follow the Holy Spirit's leading and be authentic in following through on your commitment."

   After students have made and acted on their decisions, be sensitive to students who didn't feel ready to make a commitment. Affirm and encourage them. At the first appropriate moment, invite them back into the activities.

3. *After the moment, affirm all students for making authentic commitments.* Before closing in prayer, remind students that the reason the group gets together is to ask and seek answers to spiritual questions and to strengthen individual relationships with God. Affirm all students for making

authentic decisions. Encourage those who did make commitments and those who did not. You might say something like, "I'm proud of the decisions you made today—those of you who made commitments and those of you who weren't yet ready to make commitments. If you made a commitment, I'll be praying that God gives you the strength to follow through. If you didn't make a commitment, I'll be praying that God gives you what you need to take the next step."

You now have all the basic information you need to teach an effective vision moment. However, in order for vision moments to be life-changing, you need more than information. You need an authentic relationship with Christ—one that enables you to catch his vision of how a surrendered life can be used to do great things for the Kingdom. Your transformed life demonstrates what vision moments are all about—becoming more like Christ. This is the greatest vision you can give your students.

Spiritual Growth
A Heart for God

Overview

God's greatest commandments are to love him and to love others. He loves us so much he wants us to overcome any barriers preventing us from experiencing a full relationship with him. The vision moments in this section are designed to give students a better understanding of God's loving nature and to help them realize their full potential.

1. **A Submissive Heart**

   Purpose: To encourage students to examine their openness to God's plan for their lives and challenge them to walk down the path of full devotion.

   Scripture: Psalm 127:1; Proverbs 3:5–6; Jeremiah 29:11; Romans 12:2

2. **A Moldable Heart**

   Purpose: To motivate and challenge students to allow God to mold them into the persons he desires them to be.

   Scripture: Psalm 46:10; Proverbs 2:1–5; Isaiah 64:8; Jeremiah 29:11; Matthew 14:23; Matthew 14:25–33

3. **A Renewed Heart**

   Purpose: To challenge students to examine their lives for any sin that prevents them from being a fully devoted follower of Christ.

   Scripture: Psalm 103:12; Isaiah 1:18; Colossians 3:5–10; Hebrews 8:12; James 5:16; 1 John 1:9

4. **A Replenished Heart**

   Purpose: To teach students that God is able to replenish their hearts, meet their needs, and give them the ability to serve one another.

   Scripture: Psalm 1:3; Isaiah 58:11; Matthew 20:26–28; John 4:14; John 7:38

Assessment

Directions

Use this assessment to evaluate students' needs for teaching and training regarding their spiritual growth. For each statement, place an X on the continuum closest to the response that best describes your students. Marks on the left side of the continuum indicate students would benefit from a vision moment in that area.

Students' lives are . . . A Submissive Heart
(Go to page 9.)

Conformed to the world's values	Influenced more by their friends' values than God's truth	Filled with a mix of Christian and world values	Committed to staying focused on God's truth	Transformed by God's Word and truth

Students' hearts are . . . A Moldable Heart
(Go to page 15.)

Hard and closed to God's direction	Open to the world's direction and lifestyles	Torn between the world's direction and God's direction	Open to God's Word and instruction	Completely surrendered to God's leadership

Students feel . . . A Renewed Heart
(Go to page 21.)

Imprisoned by past sins	Unable to forgive themselves	They are living two different lives	God's unconditional love and forgiveness	Total freedom and grace from God

Students have . . . A Replenished Heart
(Go to page 27.)

Very little awareness of their heart conditions	Forgotten to take time to replenish their hearts	Hearts that are neutral to God and others	Hearts that are growing in God's love	Full hearts ready to serve God and others

A SUBMISSIVE HEART

Purpose

To encourage students to examine their openness to God's plan for their lives and challenge them to walk down the path of full devotion.

Overview

This vision moment takes place outdoors, ideally in a park or forest preserve with both a wooded area and an open field. Using the many trees in the wooded area as an example of things that can crowd out God's plans and the open field as an example of having an openness to God's plans, students evaluate and identify the obstacles preventing them from following God's plan for their lives. After being challenged to decide what kind of heart they want to give to God—crowded or open—students mark their commitment by driving a tent stake into the ground with the words "Whatever you want, Lord" written on it.

Every student can walk down the path of full devotion by remembering three important steps:

Step 1: Identify the obstacles. The first step to following God is to identify those things that crowd out God's plans for our lives (Rom. 12:2).

Step 2: Realize God's potential. God can be trusted—he knows us and knows what's best for us (Ps. 127:1; Jer. 29:11).

Step 3: Choose God's leadership. Choose to follow God's lead, knowing it is the best way to live a fulfilled and exciting life (Prov. 3:5–6).

Materials

- Six-inch plastic tent stakes—one for every student and leader
- A fine-point permanent marker
- One hammer for every eight to ten students
- A sturdy bag large enough to carry the tent stakes and hammers
- A portable CD/cassette player and worship music

Preparation

1. Read through the entire moment, familiarizing yourself with the teaching points and action steps before leading your group through the moment.
2. Find a park or forest preserve where there is both a wooded area and an open area. If such a place is not available or practical in your area, choose an alternate location that enables you to contrast a crowded or cluttered space with a clear and open one. For example, an overgrown, neglected lot next to a trimmed lawn or a crowded parking lot next to an undeveloped plot of land. The teaching for this moment assumes a wooded area and an open field. If you use another location, you will need to adjust the teaching to suit your chosen location.
3. Use the permanent marker to write the following words along one side of each tent stake: "Whatever you want, Lord."
4. Place the stakes and hammers inside the bag.

Teaching Outline

Opening

PRAY—Gather students together in the wooded area and open with prayer. Ask God to reveal to each student the obstacles in their lives that are crowding out God and preventing them from pursuing a fully devoted life.

Step 1: Identify the obstacles.

TEACH—If we want to follow God's plans, we need to examine our lives for obstacles—those things that hold us back from giving our whole hearts to him. The decisions we make each day, and the consequences of those decisions, are what continuously move us toward or away from God. We don't often choose to suddenly turn away from God. Usually, we begin to take small steps away from God, which eventually lead us to a place where God is no longer part of our daily lives. The more we drift toward a worldly perspective, the tougher it is to live out the kind of life God calls us to. In some cases, we may have already drifted into rationalizing behavior that is not part of God's best plans for us. These worldly ways of looking at things are what create the barriers or obstacles that keep us from placing God first.

Look at all these trees and think of them as examples of obstacles—things that can crowd out God in our lives. These obstacles could simply be something like putting pride, fear of failure, or busyness above God, or allowing something like jealousy or an unhealthy relationship to come between us and God.

Now look again and notice that some trees are smaller than others. These represent obstacles we put in our hearts that may seem small or insignificant now but will continue to grow larger and crowd out God's will unless they're uprooted. For example, maybe you exaggerate sometimes or tell small lies or have a bad temper occasionally. These are things that can take root in our lives and become bigger problems if we don't root them out now.

ACTION—Ask students to partner with one other person and give them five minutes to walk together among the trees and to share with each other their responses to the following questions:

1. What are one or two obstacles that have the potential to grow and crowd out God's will in your life?
2. How do these obstacles affect your relationship with God?

Call the group back together after five minutes. Before asking them about some of the obstacles they came up with, share an example from your own life of something that was "no problem" at first but eventually grew into an obstacle that was not honoring to God.

After sharing your obstacle, ask students about the obstacles they came up with.

As you interact with them, refer to the setting around you to reinforce the idea that the obstacles they've identified are like trees that can grow and start to crowd out what God wants for them.

TEACH—If we aren't intentional about what we let into our hearts, our hearts can become so crowded with obstacles that we're barely able to see God and follow his will for our lives.

Step 2: Realize God's potential.

ACTION—Lead students into the open field.

TEACH—This open field represents God's unlimited potential with a heart that is free of obstacles and is wide open to his plans. An open field has that wide-open foundation for God to build on; it represents our willingness to allow God to build what he wants in our lives. We need to clear away the obstacles so God's Word has room to grow and so his plans can become clear to us.

ACTION—Ask a student to read Jeremiah 29:11: "'For I know the plans I have for you,' says the LORD. 'They are plans for good and not for disaster, to give you a future and a hope.'"

TEACH—When we give God an open heart, he can mold us into the men and women we were meant to be. The potential and possibilities are unlimited! Our willingness to identify the obstacles that keep us from following God and remove them is directly tied to our ability to become who God wants us to be.

Step 3: Choose God's leadership.

TEACH—We each have a choice: to let the obstacles in our lives grow or to get rid of them and allow God to lead and direct us. Whatever prevents you from allowing God to lead your life or prevents you from seeking his guidance is an obstacle. Proverbs 3:5–6 says, "Trust in the LORD with all your heart; do not depend on your own understanding. Seek his will in all you do, and he will direct your paths." God's promise is very clear: if we trust him and allow him to lead our lives, he will direct our paths. Imagine what God could do with your life if every day you came to him with an open heart and let him lead. What if you had a "whatever-you-want-Lord" attitude? We're going to take a few moments now to pray silently and ask God to help us remove the obstacles that keep us from saying to him, "Whatever you want, Lord."

ACTION—Allow students three or four minutes to pray silently. While they are praying, quietly place the stakes and hammers on the ground. After a few minutes, gather students together in a circle around the stakes. Show them a stake and read what is written on it: "Whatever you want, Lord."

Closing

TEACH—In the Old Testament people often marked defining moments in their lives with physical objects to remind themselves of their commitment to God and of God's commitment to them. Now we have the opportunity to do the same thing. The decision many of you just made to have a whatever-you-want-Lord attitude is a commitment that deserves to be marked in a tangible way. To do this, each of us is going to have an opportunity to take one of these tent stakes and drive it into the ground. By driving a stake, you're saying to God, "From this point on, I'm going to say, 'Whatever you want, Lord,' with everything in my life." When you feel ready, pick up a hammer and stake and drive it into the ground. We're going to do this in a spirit of worship and prayer.

ACTION—Use your portable CD/tape player and worship music to create a reflective and worshipful atmosphere. Drive your own stake into the ground first to give students an example of what to do when they are ready.

TEACH—Look around at all of the stakes in the ground. This is a powerful picture of the commitments we've made together to follow God with submissive and open hearts. Imagine what could happen for the Kingdom if we continued on a daily basis to give God a life that says, "Whatever you want, Lord." It is going to be amazing to see how God uses each of you. The decision you made today is one that can change not only your own life, but also change the lives of the friends and family you love.

PRAY—Ask God to help students remember this experience as the moment they made a commitment to say, "Whatever you want, Lord," in every area of their lives. Pray for passion and courage to live out this commitment on a daily basis.

ACTION—Ask students to remove their stakes and take them home. Tell them to put their stakes in a prominent place to remind them of their daily commitment to say, "Whatever you want, Lord."

A MOLDABLE HEART

Purpose

To motivate and challenge students to allow God to mold them into the persons he desires them to be.

Overview

Students create Play-Doh sculptures to represent the condition of their hearts for God. They reflect on who is molding their hearts— God or the world—and are challenged to create more time for God so he can mold their hearts.

We can allow God to mold us by continually asking two questions:

Vital Question 1: *What is the condition of my heart right now?* God has amazing plans for those whose hearts are open and responsive to his will and leadership (Matt. 14:25–33).

Vital Question 2: *Who is molding my heart?* There is competition for our hearts. If we do not actively seek out God and his will, we will end up being molded by the world (Isa. 64:8; Prov. 2:1–5).

Materials

- Bibles
- Photocopies of the "A Moldable Heart" handout, page 133
- Two-ounce cans of Play-Doh—one for every student
- Fine-tip permanent markers—one for every student
- All-purpose spray cleaner and paper towels for cleanup

Preparation

1. Read through the entire moment, familiarizing yourself with the teaching points and action steps before leading your group through the moment.
2. Purchase two-ounce cans of Play-Doh (available at most discount retailers and toy stores).
3. Photocopy the handout.

Teaching Outline

Opening

PRAY—Gather students together and open with prayer. Ask God to open students' eyes to the present condition of their hearts and help them identify what may be competing for their hearts' attention.

TEACH—God has great plans for us and part of those plans includes molding us into who he wants us to be. Jeremiah 29:11 says, "'For I know the plans I have for you,' says the LORD. 'They are plans for good and not for disaster, to give you a future and a hope.'" Our hearts are the center of who we are, and our hearts are what God wants us to give him so he can shape us into who he wants us to be. Isaiah 64:8 says, "And yet, LORD, you are our Father. We are the clay, and you are the potter." To help keep our hearts soft so God can mold and shape them, we need to honestly and consistently answer two vital questions.

Vital Question 1:
What is the condition of my heart right now?

TEACH—The first vital question is what is the condition of my heart right now? Asking this question helps us assess how open we are to God's will in our everyday lives. Being open to God's will means we want his truth to influence and direct us in everything from the choices and decisions we make to our relationships and how we treat others. We're going to take time right now to reflect on Vital Question 1, and then we're going to get creative with an activity that will help us express our answers to that question.

ACTION—Distribute the pens and handouts. Read out loud the directions for Vital Question 1 from the handout. Allow students enough time to mark their handouts.

When most students are done marking their handouts, distribute the cans of Play-Doh. Give students the following instructions:

- Use your can of Play-Doh to create something that expresses your answer to Vital Question 1.
- For example, creating a smiling face would represent a happy heart, one that's soft and responsive to God; jail bars might represent an imprisoned heart, one in which something is holding you back from being responsive to God; a flattened disk could represent a crushed heart, one that is hard and feels like it is impossible to be soft and responsive, etc.
- You'll have about ten minutes to complete this activity.
- Feel free to be creative!

Be sure to create an atmosphere of acceptance so students feel comfortable and able to express themselves freely.

After eight to ten minutes (when you see most students are done), call the group back together. Invite students to share with the group what they've created and how it reflects their current heart condition.

TEACH—We all know how easy it is for our hearts to drift away from being soft and responsive to God. Sometimes we get too busy to listen to him, or we want to do life on our own terms. There may be times when we are even disappointed or angry with God and we don't want to listen to him at all. God, however, is always available to us. He loves us so much and has such great plans for our lives. To keep our hearts soft, we need to listen for his direction. Consider the actions of Peter and how he listened to God's direction when the disciples were caught in a storm on the Sea of Galilee.

ACTION—Ask a student to read Matthew 14:25–33.

TEACH—Everyone in the boat was afraid, but Peter was open to God's direction in his life despite his fears. There were twelve in the boat that night:

- Eleven stayed quiet and one spoke up asking God to direct him.
- Eleven stayed safe and one stepped out, overcoming his doubts and fears.
- Eleven stayed dry and one got wet, asking God to save him.
- Eleven witnessed a miracle and one experienced it.
- Eleven were amazed at what they saw and one had his life changed forever.

Because Peter's heart was soft and responsive to God's will, he experienced a miraculous and life-changing adventure. In order for us to have faith adventures of our own, we need to keep our hearts soft and responsive with our attention focused on God. When we hear God's voice, we need to respond in faith just as Peter did. Every time we give God an obedient heart, God shapes and molds us into who he wants us to be—into who he knows we *can* be.

Vital Question 2: Who is molding my heart?

TEACH—After reflecting on Vital Question 1: What is the condition of my heart right now? we need to consider Vital Question 2: Who is molding my heart? As we saw earlier, the key to allowing God to mold us is to listen to him and follow his direction. But how do we hear or even recognize his voice within the craziness of our world? There is ongoing competition for our attention, and if we do not actively seek out God and his will, we will end up being molded by the values of the world.

ACTION—Read out loud the directions for Vital Question 2 from the handout. Allow enough time for students to complete the activity.

TEACH—Listen to just a partial list of what and who are trying to shape our values: music, TV, radio, newspapers, magazines, the Internet, friends, and teachers. We're constantly bombarded with messages from all these sources and more, and all too often they're not the same message God would have us receive. Our attitudes, desires, and actions are constantly being molded by what we hear, read, and talk about. In order to have our hearts molded by God, we need to actively search out God's guidance.

The only way to keep our hearts healthy is to make deliberate efforts to offset worldly messages by spending time with God and his Word. This is what Jesus did. He often retreated from the crowds— and even from his disciples—to be by himself and talk with God. Matthew 14:23 says, "Afterward he went up into the hills by himself to pray." We need to discipline our lives to spend time with God. Psalm 46:10 says, "'Be silent and know that I am God.'" Without spending time just listening to God, our hearts will be in real danger of drifting away from him and toward worldly things, which could cause them to become hard and unresponsive.

ACTION—Ask students to partner with one other person and give them five minutes to share their responses to the questions listed on the handout:

1. What things have the ability to draw your heart away from God?

2. Proverbs 2:1–5 says, "My child, listen to me and treasure my instructions. Tune your ears to wisdom, and concentrate on understanding. Cry out for insight and understanding. Search for them as you would for lost money or hidden treasure. Then you will understand what it means to fear the LORD, and you will gain knowledge of God." Based on this verse, what actions can you take to keep your heart soft and responsive to God?

Closing

TEACH—One truth we should always remember is found in Isaiah 64:8. Listen to what it says: "And yet, LORD, you are our Father. We are the clay, and you are the potter." God can mold us into who he wants us to be. If we are willing to allow him to shape our hearts, he will work miracles in our lives just as he did in Peter's life. But we need to keep coming back to the two vital questions: "What is the condition of my heart right now?" and "Who is molding my heart?" If we're not careful, worldly distractions will draw us away from God. So we need to ask and answer these questions honestly and regularly.

As a sign of your willingness to allow God to mold your heart from now on, take your Play-Doh creation, crunch it up, and put it back into the container. By doing this, you are saying to God, "I want *you* to mold my heart." This action is also a visual reminder that just as Play-Doh remains soft and moldable only if it is kept in its container, so our hearts remain soft and moldable only if they are kept in God's hands.

ACTION—Distribute the fine-tip markers. Instruct students to write on the outside of their Play-Doh containers: "We are the clay, and you are the potter" (Isa. 64:8).

Encourage students to put their Play-Doh containers where they will see them often and be reminded to allow God to mold their hearts.

PRAY—Thank God for his desire to shape and mold students into who he wants them to be. Ask God to help keep students' hearts soft and responsive to his will so he can mold them into who he wants them to be.

A RENEWED HEART

Purpose

To challenge students to examine their lives for any sin that prevents them from being a fully devoted follower of Christ.

Overview

This vision moment takes place outdoors. Students examine their lives for any sin that prevents them from being a fully devoted follower of Christ. They write their sin on a helium-filled white balloon and then release it as a symbol of God's willingness to forgive, remove, and forget our sins.

We can experience God's forgiveness and freedom by working through each component of the forgiveness formula:

$$N + C + R = \text{Forgiveness and Freedom.}$$

Component 1: Name your sin. Identify any sin that is holding you back from a full relationship with God (Col. 3:5–10).

Component 2: Confess your sin. Confess your sin to God and ask for forgiveness (Isa. 1:18; 1 John 1:9).

Component 3: Release your sin. God forgives and forgets confessed sin. You then need to forgive yourself and move on, knowing you are renewed and free from your sin (Ps. 103:12; Heb. 8:12; James 5:16).

Materials

- Bibles
- Plain white balloons (8 to 10 inches diameter) filled with helium and tied with thirty-six-inch pieces of kite string—one for every student, plus extras in case of breakage

- Fine-tip permanent markers—one for every student
- Worship music—either prerecorded CDs or tapes, or make arrangements for a worship leader to be present during this time

Preparation

1. Read through the entire moment, familiarizing yourself with the teaching points and action steps before leading your group through the moment.
2. Gather the balloons by loosely wrapping all the kite strings together.

Teaching Outline

Opening

PRAY—Gather students together and open with prayer. Ask God to help students experience God's amazing gift of forgiveness, which is available to everyone who asks for it. Pray that God will help students see the sins that keep them from being fully devoted followers of Christ.

TEACH—God truly desires an ongoing relationship with each of us—one that is growing and healthy. But sometimes sin gets in the way, and we start to feel disconnected from God. This time is intended to bring to the surface any sin that needs to be confronted and confessed to God. Privately, we will be going through a time of self-examination and prayer, naming our sins and confessing them to God. This will allow each of you to follow God unhindered and with your whole heart. In order to experience the freedom God wants for us, we need to ask for forgiveness. To understand how this works, it's helpful to use the forgiveness formula: Name your sin + Confess your sin + Release your sin = Forgiveness and Freedom.

Component 1: Name your sin.

TEACH—The first component of the forgiveness formula is name your sin. Don't let it hide in the shadows. Bring it out into the clear light where it can be effectively dealt with. Christ has set us free, and he doesn't want us to be entangled in our sins. We need to consistently bring our sins before Christ and humbly ask for his forgiveness.

ACTION—Ask a student to read Colossians 3:5–10: "So put to death the sinful, earthly things lurking within you. Have nothing to do with sexual sin, impurity, lust, and shameful desires. Don't be greedy for the good things of this life, for that is idolatry. God's terrible anger will come upon those who do such things. You used to do them when your life was still part of this world. But now is the time to get rid of anger, rage, malicious behavior, slander, and dirty language. Don't lie to each other, for you have stripped off your old evil nature and all its wicked deeds. In its place you have clothed yourselves with a brand-new nature that is continually being renewed as you learn more and more about Christ, who created this new nature within you."

TEACH—Although we really want to put to death those sinful things we just read about, sometimes we merely gloss over them instead. We ask God to forgive us in a general way but don't address the specific things that are displeasing to him. It can be painful to speak of specific sins because naming them forces us see sin as God must see it, and that's not a pleasant experience. It's more comfortable to keep our sins in the shadows. We also need to face the fact that our sins may have harmed others, which can be very painful. We're going to take some time now by ourselves to reflect on our lives and name our sins.

ACTION—Give students the following instructions:
- Find a quiet place nearby.
- Take a few moments to reflect on your life. Are there any areas of sin or specific sins you've been keeping in the shadows? Is anything holding you back in your relationship with God? Remember, God can handle whatever the sin might be.
- Put a name on your sin—be specific. For example: gossiping, lying, being rude to my family, stealing, addiction, drunkenness, inappropriate sexual behavior, and lust.
- You'll have about ten minutes and then we'll get back together.

You may wish to play reflective worship music in the background during this time.

While students are reflecting, retrieve the balloons and markers so they will be ready to hand out when you conclude teaching Component 2. After about ten minutes (when you see most students are done), gather the group back together.

Component 2: Confess your sins.

TEACH—Identifying and naming our sins is a good start and a necessary part of the forgiveness formula, but we can't stop there. We have to move on to Component 2 of the forgiveness formula: Confess your sins. Confessing sin enables God to forgive us. God sees our hearts and understands our desire to be released from sin. When we confess, God forgives us immediately and restores our relationship with him as if nothing had ever happened. He erases every record of our sins and makes us clean inside.

ACTION—Ask a student to read 1 John 1:9: "But if we confess our sins to him, he is faithful and just to forgive us and to cleanse us from every wrong."

Ask another student to read Isaiah 1:18: "'Come now, let us argue this out,' says the Lord. 'No matter how deep the stain of your sins, I can remove it. I can make you as clean as freshly fallen snow. Even if you are stained as red as crimson, I can make you as white as wool.'"

Distribute the balloons and markers. Explain that the white balloon represents God's promise to forgive our confessed sins and make our hearts as clean as freshly fallen snow. Give students the following instructions:

- Find a quiet place nearby.
- Take a few moments to pray and confess your sins to God. Remember how much God loves you and wants to forgive and forget your sins.
- Once you have confessed your sin, write it on your balloon. No one else will see what you've written.
- You'll have about ten minutes.

You may wish to play reflective worship music in the background during this time.

After eight to ten minutes (when you see most students are done), call the group back together. Affirm their decisions to name and confess these sins to God.

PRAY—Mark the significance of this moment with prayer. Thank God for the miracle of forgiving and forgetting sin. Ask God to now begin healing students' hearts and minds so they can enjoy a restored relationship with Christ.

Component 3: Release your sins.

TEACH—Component 3 in the forgiveness formula is release your sins. This is important. Listen to Psalm 103:12: "He has removed our rebellious acts as far away as the east is from the west." And Hebrews 8:12 says, "I will forgive their wrongdoings, and I will never again remember their sins." Isn't that great news! After we confess our sins, God gets rid of them. He removes them and no longer remembers them. They are as far away from us "as the east is from the west." God doesn't want you to feel weighed down by sins he's forgiven. But sometimes it's harder for us to forgive and release ourselves. We feel remorse or guilt or become discouraged when we realize what we've done. Sometimes there are long-term consequences of our actions. But we need to release our confessed sin so it can't do any more damage, and so it won't hinder us any longer. We need to let God take the sin away from us. That is the freedom Christ bought for us.

ACTION—Instruct students to release their balloons. Encourage them to watch the balloons drift upward. Begin teaching the following section while the balloons are still in sight.

TEACH—Watching these balloons drift up and away visually represents how God separates us from our sins. We need to do the same. We need to release the feelings of guilt and shame we have about our sins. As the balloons continue to float away, remember that you are released and forgiven from your sins. What a fantastic picture of how much God loves and cares for us!

ACTION—Pause for a moment. In silence, allow students to continue watching the balloons drift away so this picture of God's forgiveness and freedom sinks into their hearts and minds. After the balloons are out of sight, gather students back together.

Closing

TEACH—We've gone through the three components of the forgiveness formula and now we have the result, which equals forgiveness and freedom. God wants us to always feel the freedom of an unhindered relationship with him. He wants us to continually work through this forgiveness formula so we may enjoy the freedom he has waiting for us. Remember the formula with the initials N, C, R:

Name + Confess + Release = Forgiveness and Freedom

To help keep ourselves free from sin we need to lean on one another and help each other out. It is a good idea to have one or two close, trusted friends with whom we can share our temptations, confess our sins, and encourage each other to remember God's truth. Sharing our struggles and praying for one another is a healthy, God-honoring thing to do. James 5:16 says, "Confess your sins to each other and pray for each other so that you may be healed. The earnest prayer of a righteous person has great power and wonderful results." Take a moment right now and think of a Christian friend or a leader you trust.

(Pause for a moment to allow students to do this.)

Talk to that person this week and ask them to be your accountability partner and meet with you on a regular basis. Having accountability in your life is a safeguard to keep you fully devoted to God.

PRAY—Thank God for his love and forgiveness and ask him to give students the strength to continue on a path of naming, confessing, and releasing their sins. Ask him to bring people into students' lives to help them be reminded of God's truth and stay accountable so they can enjoy a full and unhindered relationship with him.

VISION MOMENT 4

A REPLENISHED HEART

Purpose

To teach students that God is able to replenish their hearts, meet their needs, and give them the ability to serve one another.

Overview

This vision moment can take place indoors or outdoors. Students use the water level in a drinking glass to represent their present spiritual condition. They then use a pitcher of water to fill each others' glasses as a symbol of God's ability to refill our spiritual lives and to demonstrate how he uses our service to one another to express his love for us.

We can allow God to replenish our hearts and we can serve one another by accepting three biblical facts.

Fact 1: Jesus is the only one who can satisfy the needs of our hearts. He is the only one who can fill our lives with living water (John 7:38; John 4:14).

Fact 2: God is able to fill our hearts with purpose and satisfy our needs. The result is that we are filled to overflowing (Ps. 1:3; Isa. 58:11).

Fact 3: God expects his followers to serve one another. We are to follow Christ's example by serving each other (Matt. 20:26–28).

Materials

- Photocopies of "A Replenished Heart" handout, page 134
- Pens/pencils—one for every student

- Clear drinking glasses filled with water—one for every student and leader
- A clear pitcher, large enough to hold all the water from the drinking glasses (depending on the number of students, you may need additional pitchers)
- Towels for cleanup

Preparation

1. Read through the entire moment, familiarizing yourself with the teaching points and action steps before leading your group through the moment.
2. Photocopy the handout.
3. Select a pitcher large enough to fill all of the glasses and still have some water left over. If you have more than eight to ten students, break them into smaller groups and use one pitcher for each small group.
4. Fill the pitcher(s) with water.
5. Use the filled pitcher(s) to fill every glass with water but not to the brim. Some water should remain in the pitcher when all the glasses are filled.
6. Set the pitcher and the water-filled glasses in the center of the circle where the group will be sitting.

Teaching Outline

Opening

PRAY—Gather students together in a circle around the pitcher and glasses and open with prayer. Ask God to teach students how to fill their hearts and lives with purpose and love. Pray that God will help students see how they can serve one another and become more like Christ.

ACTION—Instruct students to each take one glass of water from the center and place it in front of them.

TEACH—Think of the water in your glass as a symbol of your spiritual life. A glass full of water represents a life that is spiritually full and committed to God. A glass with little water represents a life that feels empty and maybe even distant from God. What would cause a life that is spiritually full—like your glasses—to lose water and become spiritually empty?

ACTION—Allow several students to respond before continuing. Possible responses:
- Various trials like a death in the family or a divorce
- Problems at home
- A life that is very busy or filled with pressure about the future or relationships
- Not spending time alone with God or reading the Bible
- A pattern of unconfessed sin

TEACH—As Christ-followers, we want our lives to be spiritually full so we can feel close to God and live out his plans for us. However, there are times when we make poor decisions or when circumstances completely out of our control drain us and leave us feeling spiritually empty.

All of us are at different levels in our spiritual lives—someplace between empty and full. We're going to use the water in our glasses to represent how full we are spiritually. In just a moment, you'll pick up your glass and pour some of the water into the pitcher. The amount of water left in your glass represents where you are spiritually. If your heart and spiritual life feel completely empty, pour all the water into the pitcher. If your heart feels half empty, pour half the water into the pitcher. If your heart feels full, you may not want to pour out any water. After you've got the right water level, we'll have a chance to talk about the level we chose.

ACTION—Set an example by being the first to pour the water from your glass into the pitcher. Explain why you are at the level you chose. Continue around the circle one at a time, until every student has poured water into the pitcher and explained where he or she is spiritually.

Distribute the handouts.

Fact 1: Jesus is the only one who can satisfy the needs of our hearts.

TEACH—As you can see by the different amounts of water in our glasses, we are all at different levels in our spiritual lives. But wherever we are, all of us could use some refilling. To get a clearer picture of what it means to be spiritually filled, we're going to look at three biblical facts. The first fact is Jesus is the only one who can satisfy the needs of our hearts. John 7:38 says, "'If you believe in me, come and drink! For the Scriptures declare that rivers of living water will flow out from within.'" And John 4:14 says, "'But the water I give them takes away thirst altogether. It becomes a perpetual spring within them, giving them eternal life.'"

We're going to take a few minutes to talk about what it means to "drink" Jesus into our lives.

ACTION—Ask students to gather in groups of three or four and give them seven to ten minutes to share their responses to the questions listed on the handout:
1. What does Jesus have the ability to do for empty lives?
2. What does he ask us to do in order to drink in his living water?

Call the group back together after seven to ten minutes.

Fact 2: God is able to fill our hearts with purpose and satisfy our needs.

TEACH—The second biblical fact about being spiritually filled is that God is able to fill our hearts with purpose and satisfy our needs. Psalm 1:3 says, "They are like trees planted along the riverbank, bearing fruit each season without fail. Their leaves never wither, and in all they do, they prosper." Isaiah 58:11 says, "The LORD will guide you continually, watering your life when you are dry and keeping you healthy, too. You will be like a well-watered garden, like an ever-flowing spring."

These passages make it very clear that the result of letting God guide our lives is that our lives will be filled to overflowing. The world also gives advice on how to fill our lives. The results, however, are much different from God's. Let's take a few minutes to discuss this.

ACTION—Ask students to partner with one other person and give them five minutes to share their responses to the questions listed on the handout:
1. What are some things the world tells you will fill your life (for example, a lot of money, sex, success)?
2. What have you seen to be the result when people try to fill their lives with the world's answers instead of God's truth?
3. According to Psalm 1:3 and Isaiah 58:11, what are the results of a life filled by God?

Call the group back together after five minutes.

Fact 3: God expects his followers to serve one another.

TEACH—The world cannot come close to God's promise of filling our lives with purpose and meeting our needs. Not only does God fill our lives, but he gives us the ability to help others fill their lives as well. One way he chooses to do this is by the third biblical fact: God *expects* his followers to serve one another. Jesus says in Matthew 20:26–28, "But among you it should be quite different. Whoever wants to be a leader among you must be your servant, and whoever wants to be first must become your slave. For even I, the Son of Man, came here not to be served but to serve others, and to give my life as a ransom for many." God's desire is to serve us, and for us to serve one another!

ACTION—Take the pitcher and fill the glass of the student to your left. As you fill his or her glass say, "God is able to fill your life."

TEACH—God has asked us to be servants to one another. Let this pitcher of water represent God's endless love and his ability to meet our needs. Let the pouring of water into each others' glasses be a reminder of how God uses people like you and me to serve one another with his love. Now it's your turn to take the pitcher and, one at a time, fill the glass of the person on your left. As you fill the glass, say, "God is able to fill your life." Then pass the pitcher to the next person until everyone's glass is full.

ACTION—Wait for every glass to be filled before proceeding.

TEACH—God's love is endless! He has an unlimited ability to meet our needs. God wants all of us to show his love to each other. This week look for practical ways to serve one another. You can do this with kind words, a listening heart, a simple prayer, or a helping hand—all of these actions show God's love to others and help to keep our hearts full. The water you hold in your hands represents your commitment to love God and to love others with a full heart.

Do you know someone whose heart is half empty and could use some filling with God's love? Who could you serve this week in a practical way? Maybe you could even partner with a friend to serve someone. Let's take a few minutes individually to really think about this and make it practical. At the end of the handout is a place for you to write in the name of one person and how you can serve them this week. Take a few minutes now to fill this out.

ACTION—Distribute the pens/pencils. After a few minutes (when you see most students are done), call the group back together.

Closing

TEACH—We have learned three powerful biblical facts about God's ability to replenish our hearts and how God also gives us the ability to help others in their times of need. Now it's up to us to take these facts and make them real in our lives. We need to live in such a way that we know when our lives are becoming spiritually empty so we can slow down enough to let God fill our hearts. We need to live with an attitude that's willing to serve others, knowing that it is pleasing God when we do this.

PRAY—Thank God for always being willing and able to fill our hearts with his living water. Thank him for his purpose and blessing in our lives. Ask God to help students follow through on their commitment this week to serve the person whose name they wrote down on the handout.

Part 2

Community
Caring for Each Other

Overview

In Acts 2 we see a picture of the early church and how it was committed to building a community of believers who loved God and loved others. The vision moments in this section are designed to help you focus on building a student ministry filled with Christ-followers who demonstrate an Acts 2 commitment to becoming a biblically functioning community.

5. **Who You Are**
   Purpose: To challenge students to be intentional about building each other up with encouragement.
   Scripture: Psalm 139:13–14; Romans 1:12; Romans 12:2; Philippians 1:6; 1 Thessalonians 5:11

6. **Reflections**
   Purpose: To challenge students to be individuals who reflect Christ and encourage others to do the same.
   Scripture: Proverbs 27:17; Daniel 12:3; Matthew 5:16; Mark 12:30; Romans 1:12; Romans 14:19; Galatians 5:22–23

7. **Say the Words**
   Purpose: To raise the value of Christian friends who encourage, support, and keep each other accountable to become fully devoted followers of Christ.
   Scripture: Proverbs 27:17; Ecclesiastes 4:9–12; Hebrews 3:13

8. **A 2:14 Attitude**
   Purpose: To challenge students to develop a positive, Christlike attitude.
   Scripture: Philippians 2:4; Philippians 2:5; Philippians 2:6–8; Philippians 2:7; Philippians 2:8; Philippians 2:14

Assessment

Directions

Use this assessment to evaluate students' needs for teaching and training in what it means to care for others and build community. For each statement, place an *X* on the continuum closest to the response that best describes your students. Marks on the left side of the continuum indicate students would benefit from a vision moment in that area.

In our student ministry . . .   Who You Are
(Go to page 35.)

Students do not know who God made them to be	Students do not care about who they are in God	Students are open to learning about who they are in God	Students are learning more about who God made them to be	Students know who they are in God

In our student ministry . . .   Reflections
(Go to page 41.)

Students reflect worldly values more than they reflect Christlike values	Students reflect some Christlike values	Students reflect both worldly values and Christlike values	Students desire to reflect more Christlike values	Students help each other reflect Christlike values

In our student ministry . . .   Say the Words
(Go to page 47.)

Students never encourage each other	Students rarely see the need for encouragement	Students know the value of encouragement	Students often say encouraging words to each other	Students actively encourage each other

In our student ministry . . .   A 2:14 Attitude
(Go to page 54.)

Students have a negative attitude	Students have a "what's-in-it-for-me?" attitude	Students try to have a positive attitude	Students have an attitude that honors others	Students have a Christlike attitude

WHO YOU ARE

Purpose

To challenge students to be intentional about building each other up with encouragement.

Overview

This moment can take place indoors or outdoors. Students are taught who they are from God's perspective. They are reminded of who they are becoming and the role they play in building others up through words of encouragement. They offer public words of encouragement to one another and are challenged to continue this practice on a regular basis.

We can all encourage and build up others with two biblical reminders:

Reminder 1: Remember who you are. We have been uniquely made—wonderfully complex masterpieces of God's handiwork (Ps. 139:13–14).

Reminder 2: Remember who you are becoming. We are continually in the process of becoming more like Christ, and we can contribute to this process in others by regularly encouraging one another (Rom. 12:2; Rom. 1:12; Phil. 1:6).

Materials

- Bibles
- Photocopies of the "Who You Are" handout, page 135

Preparation

1. Read through the entire moment, familiarizing yourself with the teaching points and action steps before leading your group through the moment.
2. Photocopy the handout.

Teaching Outline

Opening

PRAY—Gather students together and open with prayer. Ask God to remind students of the truths in Scripture about how precious we are to him. Pray that God would give students courage to open up and encourage each other so they might grow closer as a group and be motivated to pursue God more fully.

TEACH—God desires us to learn how to build each other up, and he wants us to strengthen our youth ministry. We can do that by keeping in mind two reminders: "Remember who you are" and "Remember who you are becoming." God wants to constantly remind each one of us about these truths so we might be encouraged to follow him more fully.

Reminder 1: Remember who you are.

TEACH—Reminder 1 is remember who you are. The Bible teaches that we have been uniquely made, that we are wonderfully complex masterpieces of God's handiwork. In the world we live in, we all have multiple roles to fulfill—we are sons and daughters, brothers and sisters, students, athletes, club members, employees, musicians, friends, etc. With all of these roles and the expectations they carry, it's easy to lose sight of who we really are in God's eyes.

God never wants us to forget who we are to him. Psalm 139:13–14 describes who God made us to be. It says, "You made all the delicate, inner parts of my body and knit me together in my mother's womb. Thank you for making me so wonderfully complex! Your workmanship is marvelous—and how well I know it." God has

made us each unique. Although we have a variety of roles and responsibilities, we need to remember that within these roles we first belong
to God. Remembering this truth brings us hope and assurance that we
are loved and cared for—that we are an important part of the community of believers because God has made us unique and chosen us
to be his beloved.

ACTION—Distribute the handout. Ask students to take turns
reading a verse out loud. Continue until all the verses have been
read.

Ask students to break into groups of three or four and give them
seven to ten minutes to share the verse that encourages them most
and why it is meaningful to them. After seven to ten minutes (when
you see most students are done), call them back together.

Reminder 2: Remember who you are becoming.

TEACH—Reminder 2 is remember who you are becoming. It is
great to hear about who we are in Christ—about the wonderful head
start God has given us. But it is also good to hear about who we are
becoming. We are continually in the process of becoming even more
like Christ, and we can contribute to this process in others by the
regular practice of encouraging one another in that effort.

Romans 12:2 says, "Don't copy the behavior and customs of this
world, but let God transform you into a new person by changing the
way you think. Then you will know what God wants you to do and
you will know how good and pleasing and perfect his will really is."
We are under construction. God is at work changing us—if we let
him. When we look at where we are in this process, too often we
focus on the negatives—where we messed up, where we're not hit-
ting the mark, what we need to improve. Although it's good to be
honest about our shortcomings, we also need to acknowledge where
we are growing and making progress. And we can encourage one
another when we acknowledge growth and progress.

ACTION—Ask a student to read Romans 1:12: "I'm eager to
encourage you in your faith, but I also want to be encouraged by yours.
In this way, each of us will be a blessing to the other."

TEACH—This verse teaches the value of both giving and receiving encouragement. Through encouragement we can build each other up, help each other grow, strengthen our relationships, and build our community.

In the early church, a man named Joseph was known as an encourager. Encouragement was such an integral part of who he was that he was given the nickname Barnabas, which means "son of encouragement." His encouragement is thought to have been a key factor in the spiritual growth of the apostle Paul. We need to let the example of Barnabas challenge and encourage us because we never know when a simple, encouraging word might lift up a fellow Christian or inspire him to continue with his spiritual growth.

ACTION—Ask a student to read Philippians 1:6: "And I am sure that God, who began the good work within you, will continue his work until it is finally finished on that day when Christ Jesus comes back again."

TEACH—In this verse Paul explained that God is at work in each of us for the rest of our lives. That's pretty encouraging! As we grow in Christ, he grows in us. As this growth process continues, Christ increasingly replaces our negative motives, feelings, and beliefs with his power, love, and peace. While Christ is working in us, it is good to hear encouragement from others. We all can play a critical role in the growth of each other by being faithful encouragers of how we see God working in each of our lives.

We're going to take some time right now as a group to practice encouraging each other. One at a time, I want you to encourage at least one person by completing this sentence out loud, "I see you becoming . . ." Finish the sentence with a statement about how you have seen this person becoming more like Christ. For example, "I see you becoming more patient when you're around your family." Or "I see you becoming more compassionate for our friends who are not Christ-followers."

ACTION—Set the example by being the first to share with one or two students how you have seen changes take place in their lives and who you see them becoming. Note: To prevent any students from being inadvertently left out, watch carefully for students who are not being encouraged and take the initiative to say something to them. Do not wait until the end to offer your encouragement—this will tend to draw attention to them—but do it while the students are sharing. You may want to ask another leader to help watch for this.

When everyone has been encouraged, help students process their experiences by asking them to share their observations and feelings about giving and receiving encouragement. Ask:

- What was it like to give encouragement?
- What was it like to receive encouragement?

Allow several students to share before moving on.

Closing

TEACH—First Thessalonians 5:11 says, "So encourage each other and build each other up, just as you are already doing." Don't let this time of encouragement we experienced be a one-time event. Encouragement is something we need to practice continually—one on one, in small groups, in church, at school, everywhere we go. Remembering who we are in Christ, and who we are in the process of becoming, will help us stay focused, encouraged, and better prepared to follow him fully.

There are many ways to encourage each other, so we need to keep finding new ways to do so. As one final act of encouragement, we're going to pray for each other. Praying for someone is one of the deepest ways we can show our care and support. We're going to first have the guys stand in the middle, and the girls will gather around in a circle and pray for them. Then we'll have the girls in the middle, and the guys will gather around in a circle and pray for them.

ACTION—Instruct the guys to move toward the middle and have the girls gather around them. Select a few girls and ask them to pray that the guys would become men of God who are sensitive to God's leadings in their lives and that they will never forget who they are and who they are becoming. Next have the girls move into the middle and have the guys gather around them. Select a few guys and ask them to pray that the girls would become women of God who are sensitive to

God's leadings in their lives and that they will never forget who they are and who they are becoming.

PRAY—Close in prayer, thanking God for how he has made each student so uniquely wonderful. Ask God to give students the proper perspective on who they are and who they are becoming in him. Pray that God would give students a passion in their hearts to become a Barnabas.

VISION MOMENT 6

REFLECTIONS

Purpose

To challenge students to be individuals who reflect Christ and encourage others to do the same.

Overview

This moment can be done indoors or outdoors. Using pieces of aluminum foil as a symbol of their desire to reflect Christlike qualities, students write personal notes on the foil describing how they see Christ reflected in each others' lives.

We can all reflect Christ in our lives and encourage others to do the same by practicing two healthy building habits:

Healthy Habit 1: Build in. Building in means developing lifelong patterns of personal growth that deepen our relationship with Christ. The gradual and ongoing change that results from these patterns helps us to become clearer reflections of Christ (Mark 12:30).

Healthy Habit 2: Build up. Building up means encouraging others. Encouragement is a powerful force that motivates people to continue developing Christlike patterns, becoming clearer reflections of Christ (Prov. 27:17; Matt. 5:16; Rom. 1:12; Rom. 14:19).

Materials

- Bibles
- Aluminum foil
- Scissors
- Masking tape

- A wide-tip permanent marker
- Fine-tip permanent markers—one for every student
- A table or other surface for students to write on if there is not a table or floor available (for example, if done outdoors)

Optional

- Poster board
- Easel
- CD/tape player and contemplative, instrumental worship music

Preparation

1. Read through the entire moment, familiarizing yourself with the teaching points and action steps before leading your group through the moment.
2. On a poster-size sheet of aluminum foil, use the wide-tip marker to write out in large print the text of Galatians 5:22–23: "But when the Holy Spirit controls our lives, he will produce this kind of fruit in us: love, joy, peace, patience, kindness, goodness, faithfulness, gentleness, and self-control." Before meeting with students, hang the foil where everyone will be able to see it. Tape it to a wall or to a poster board placed on an easel.
3. Cut letter-size (approximately 8½ by 11 inches) pieces of aluminum foil—one for every student.
4. Cut wallet-photo-size (approximately two inches by two inches) pieces of aluminum foil—one for every student.

Teaching Outline

Opening

PRAY—Gather students together and open with prayer. Thank God for his desire to have a personal relationship with every student. Ask God to help students see how the power of encouragement can build up those around them.

TEACH—Daniel 12:3 says, "Those who are wise will shine as bright as the sky, and those who turn many to righteousness will shine like stars forever." We all want to shine brightly for Christ, and the way to shine is simple—we need to know Christ better. The more we know about Christ, the better we will be able to act like him. The Bible says we should be examples of Christ. This is the way we can shine like the stars, reflecting Christ to others. To do this we need to practice two healthy building habits: *build in* patterns of personal growth and *build up* others.

Healthy Habit 1: Build in.

TEACH—To reflect Christ, the first healthy habit we need to develop is build in. We need to build in patterns of personal growth that will help us develop Christlike qualities. In order for us to develop these qualities, we need to know something about Christ. We need to know what he stood for, what he valued, what he loved, what he despised. We need to continually learn more about Christ and about developing our relationship with him.

ACTION—Ask a student to read Mark 12:30: "'You must love the Lord your God with all your heart, all your soul, all your mind, and all your strength.'"

TEACH—God's number-one desire is that we get this right. When we love God and keep him first in every area of our lives, he begins to change us so we gradually become clearer reflections of him. This is an ongoing process, one that never really ends because there is always more to experience with Christ. In this lifelong spiritual journey, we will be able to see signs of how we are doing. God gives us clear signposts to look for—those things that start to show up in our lives as we actively pursue him. Let's take a look at how the Bible describes some of these signposts of growth and assess how we are doing with reflecting Christ.

ACTION—Give students the following instructions:
• Read Galatians 5:22–23 silently.

- Take a few moments to reflect on your life and identify any areas where you could be a clearer reflection of Christ. For example, "I need to work on being more patient with my younger brother or sister." Or "I need to show more self-control in my relationship with my boyfriend/girlfriend."
- You'll have about five minutes and then we'll come back together.

You may choose to play contemplative, instrumental worship music during this time.

After about five minutes, call the group back together. Ask students to gather in groups of three or four and share their thoughts about how they are or are not reflecting Christ using Galatians 5:22–23 as the signposts for evaluating themselves.

Healthy Habit 2: Build up

ACTION—Ask a student to read Matthew 5:16: "'In the same way, let your good deeds shine out for all to see, so that everyone will praise your heavenly Father.'"

TEACH—As this verse says, we want our good deeds to bring praise to God, not to ourselves, but encouraging words give us the motivation to keep living God-honoring lives. This is the second healthy habit: build up. The Bible tells us we should encourage one another continually. This means building each other up, not tearing each other down. Encouraging words confirm we are doing things right and give us hope and courage to keep going. Listen to Proverbs 27:17: "As iron sharpens iron, a friend sharpens a friend." We need to sharpen each other's faith and character. This means we're always on the lookout for others to do something right. We want to catch them in the act of doing something good and encourage them to keep at it.

ACTION—Ask a student to read Romans 1:12: "I'm eager to encourage you in your faith, but I also want to be encouraged by yours. In this way, each of us will be a blessing to the other."

TEACH—The apostle Paul knew the importance of encouragement—both giving it and receiving it. He knew the Christians he ministered to needed to be encouraged at all times to overcome the dangerous situations and messages they encountered every day.

We face dangerous situations and messages from the world today just like the early Christians did. It's easy to forget how important we are to God because we don't hear that message very often. We are God's messengers to each other. God wants us to be his voice of encouragement to those around us. Listen to Romans 14:19: "So then, let us aim for harmony in the church and try to build each other up." Every day we have opportunities to either reflect or deflect Christ's image. One aspect of reflecting Christ's image is encouraging others—Jesus encouraged others throughout his lifetime, inspiring people and giving them hope. We need to follow this example.

ACTION—Distribute the letter-size pieces of aluminum foil and fine-tip permanent markers. Give students the following instructions:
- Partner with one other person.
- Take a moment to think about what you have heard your partner say or seen him or her do that reflects Christ.
- Write a note to your partner on your piece of foil. Tell your partner how he or she reflects Christ by completing this sentence: "You have reflected Christ by . . ."
- Don't share your note with your partner yet. In a few minutes we'll share our notes together as a group.
- You'll have about five minutes.

After five to seven minutes (when you see most students are done), gather the group back together. One by one, go around the group and have the students read aloud the notes they wrote to their partners. Ask students to give the notes to their partners to keep.

Closing

TEACH—Paul said, "So encourage each other and build each other up, just as you are already doing" (1 Thess. 5:11). Continue to reflect Christ to those around you so that through your actions you may encourage reflecting Christ to others. Continue encouraging one another by trying to catch each other doing something right. What is written on your piece of foil is evidence of how someone else has seen you reflecting Christ. Be encouraged! This is proof you are becoming more like Christ.

ACTION—Distribute the wallet-size pieces of foil. Read again Matthew 5:16: "'In the same way, let your good deeds shine out for all to see, so that everyone will praise your heavenly Father.'" Give students the following instructions:

- Write "Matthew 5:16" on the foil.
- Put the foil someplace you will see it every day—in your wallet, purse, locker, or a prominent place in your room.

TEACH—This small piece of foil is your reminder that you are called to represent and reflect Christ to the world around you. We need to do all we can to pursue a deep relationship with Christ and we also need to daily be encouraging each other to reflect Christ to those around us.

PRAY—Ask God to help students become individuals who reflect Christ in their daily lives and who also eagerly encourage one another to do the same.

VISION MOMENT 7

SAY THE WORDS

Purpose

To raise the value of Christian friends who encourage, support, and keep each other accountable to become fully devoted followers of Christ.

Overview

This vision moment can be done indoors or outdoors. Utilizing carabiners—oblong metal rings used for mountain climbing—students literally "hook up" in groups of three. This illustrates the strength of Christian friendships and how they help us become more like Christ.

We can raise the value of encouragement, support, and accountability in Christian friendships by remembering three biblical truths:

Truth 1: Words are powerful. Words have a tremendous capacity to encourage us and keep us on track (Heb. 3:13).

Truth 2: Two are better than one. It is good to have Christian friends to support us in times of need (Eccles. 4:9–12).

Truth 3: Iron sharpens iron. God expects us to learn from one another and hold each other accountable (Prov. 27:17).

Materials

- Bibles
- Photocopies of the "Say the Words" handout, page 136
- Carabiners—one for every student and leader
- Kite string (optional)

Preparation

1. Read through the entire moment, familiarizing yourself with the teaching points and action steps before leading your group through the moment.
2. Photocopy the handout.

Teaching Outline

Opening

PRAY—Gather students together in a circle and open with prayer. Thank God for Christian friends. Ask God to teach students how to support and encourage one another so they can become a student ministry connected to each other by truth and love.

ACTION—Distribute handouts.

TEACH—Good Christian friendships are gifts that should not be taken for granted. To have good friends, we need to be good friends. In this study, we are going to learn three truths from God's Word that will help us build strong Christian friendships.

Truth 1: Words are powerful.

TEACH—The first truth is words are powerful. When you were a kid, did you ever use little sayings to help you win arguments? Things like: "I'm rubber, you're glue; everything you say bounces off of me and sticks to you!" Or maybe: "Sticks and stones may break my bones, but words can never hurt me." These are catchy little phrases, but the truth is that words *do* hurt. They really can impact us in negative ways. Words can also make us really happy. When we get a compliment or other positive feedback, it can make our day. God knows words are powerful and that words have the ability to change lives. That's why he tells us to speak words of encouragement to one another every day.

ACTION—Ask a student to read Hebrews 3:13: "But encourage one another daily, as long as it is called Today, so that none of you may be hardened by sin's deceitfulness" (NIV).

TEACH—As this verse points out, we should always be ready to give a word of encouragement. Getting a compliment, hearing a kind word at the right moment, or being acknowledged for something done well can have an amazing impact on us—especially if we are feeling down or discouraged. It doesn't take much to make a positive difference in someone's day—or maybe even his or her life.

We're going to take a few minutes to talk about the power of encouragement.

ACTION—Ask students to partner with one other person and give them five minutes to share their responses to the questions for Truth 1 listed on the handout:

- Share a time when you were encouraged at just the right time with the right words from a Christian friend.
- Why was your friend's encouragement meaningful to you? How did it make you feel?

After five minutes, call the group back together. Invite a few students to share their stories with the group before proceeding.

Truth 2: Two are better than one.

TEACH—If we want to raise the value of encouragement, the second truth to remember is that two are better than one. It feels good to know someone is there for you, believing in you, especially when you are down or feel very alone. Knowing someone is there when you need him or her is a great gift. God knows this is an important truth in building a strong community among Christian friends.

ACTION—Ask a student to read Ecclesiastes 4:9–12: "Two people can accomplish more than twice as much as one; they get a better return for their labor. If one person falls, the other can reach out and help. But people who are alone when they fall are in real trouble. And on a cold night, two under the same blanket can gain warmth from each other. But how can one be warm alone? A person standing alone can be attacked and defeated, but two can stand back-to-back and conquer. Three are even better, for a triple-braided cord is not easily broken."

TEACH—All of us have probably experienced a time when this truth became very real to us—a time when someone was there for us when we really needed help. We're going to take some time to share together an experience of when someone was there for us in a time of need.

ACTION—Ask students to partner with one other person—someone different than before—and give them five minutes to share their responses to the questions for Truth 2 listed on the handout:
- Share a time when someone was there for you when you were in need.
- How did it make you feel?
- How did it change your attitude or situation?

After five minutes, call the group back together. Invite a few students to share their stories with the group before proceeding.

TEACH—I'm sure you heard some great stories of how important it is to have friends around in a time of need. Listen again to Ecclesiastes 4:12: "A person standing alone can be attacked and defeated, but two can stand back-to-back and conquer. Three are even better, for a triple-braided cord is not easily broken." What does this teach us about the importance of Christian friendships when it comes to staying strong for God?

ACTION—Solicit three or four responses. Possible responses include:
- Sometimes it's hard to stand alone for your faith.
- We all make mistakes, and when we do it's important to have a friend to help us get back up and keep trying.
- You can do much more for God as a group than you can alone.

Option: A good way to illustrate this truth is to take a length of kite string, wrap it between your index fingers, and then break it. Next, take three lengths of kite string, wrap them between your index fingers, and then try to break them. The three strings together will be much more difficult to break.

TEACH—It is not wise to stand alone. "Two are better than one" is a powerful truth for building strong friendships. We need our Christian friendships to encourage and support us.

Truth 3: Iron sharpens iron.

TEACH—The third truth for building strong Christian friendships is iron sharpens iron.

ACTION—Ask a student to read Proverbs 27:17: "As iron sharpens iron, a friend sharpens a friend."

TEACH—Just as a blacksmith sharpens a piece of metal into a sword, God wants us to keep each other sharp in our Christian walk. He knows it is important for us not only to hear words of encouragement and have someone support us when we're down, but also to have friends who speak truth to us. We sharpen each other when we speak words of truth that redirect us back to a path of full devotion to Christ. To be sharpened by someone's words of truth can be difficult. We don't like to be corrected or told we are wrong. But when someone comes to us in a true spirit of love, not afraid to sharpen us with words that help us become who God wants us to be, it's a precious gift we need to hang onto. It's also a gift we need to be willing to give others. We're going to take some time to talk about how this way of sharpening each other can be lived out in our relationships.

ACTION—Ask students to partner with one other person—someone different than before—and give them five to seven minutes to share their responses to the questions for Truth 3 on the handout:
- Share a time when you received correction—words of truth—from a friend. How open were you to the correction? How did you feel afterward? What difference did it make in your life?
- Share a time when you corrected a friend with words of truth. Was it difficult for you? Why or why not? How did the person respond?

After five to seven minutes, call the group back together. Invite a few students to share their experiences with the group before proceeding.

TEACH—If we build a community of friends like this, we will all be amazed at what God can do through our student ministry. I believe our non-Christian friends would want to be a part of a community like this. It all starts with staying committed to the truths we've been talking about. We want to become a community of Christian friends who:

- Encourage one another.
- Support and help each other.
- Are not afraid to sharpen one another with words of truth.

ACTION—Hold up a carabiner and ask: "Does anyone know what this is and what it's used for?" Allow several students to respond.

TEACH—This is a carabiner; it's most often used for mountain climbing. It hooks up to a rope support system that is the climber's lifeline. If climbers are tethered to the ropes with a carabiner, they can't fall—even if they lose their grip or their footing. That's what Christian community is when it's at its best—a place where being tethered to each other keeps us from falling even when we stumble or make mistakes. This is a great picture of what our ministry can become. A place where we:

- Connect the truth from God's Word to our lives.
- Build Christian relationships so we're not alone.
- Speak words of truth from hearts of love.
- Are committed to becoming an authentic community of Christ-followers.

ACTION—Ask students to break into groups of three and sit on the floor. Distribute the carabiners. Instruct students to hook the three carabiners together and then to hold on to one end of their carabiner.

TEACH—We're going to take time to pray for one another. We'll do this in a way that illustrates what we've been talking about—connecting together to encourage, support, and sharpen each other. Don't miss the visual picture of what we're about to do—of our student ministry being connected together by Christian relationships—a community committed to loving God and loving others. I want you to pray together, asking God to help us be a ministry that really is connected to each other, that supports one another, that encourages each other, and that sharpens one another. Thank God for the opportunity we have to build a strong student ministry community.

ACTION—After five to seven minutes, call the group back together. Instruct students to disconnect the carabiners and stand up.

Closing

TEACH—What we just did illustrates the values of encouragement, support, and accountability we need to live out in our ministry throughout the year. Use your carabiner as a key ring so it's always with you. Every time you look at it, remember to encourage each other, to help each other, and to sharpen one another. We can be known as a place connected together by God's truth, where we love and encourage each other; a place where our non-Christian friends want to come and be a part of what we have; a place where this generation loves God and loves others.

PRAY—Ask God to help students be accountable to one another, encourage one another, and sharpen each other with words of love so they can become a community that loves God and loves others.

VISION MOMENT 8

A 2:14 ATTITUDE

Purpose

To challenge students to develop a positive, Christlike attitude.

Overview

This vision moment can take place indoors or outdoors. After reviewing the qualities Jesus lived out—service, humility, and obedience—students do a short self-evaluation on how their lives reflect those same qualities. They are challenged to adopt a "2:14 attitude"—the attitude of one willing to do everything without complaining or arguing. Students who accept the challenge sign a commitment pledge.

We can improve our attitude by remembering three qualities of Christ's life:

Quality 1: Christ was a servant. Jesus didn't come to do his own will; he came to serve others (Phil. 2:4).

Quality 2: Christ was humble. Jesus became less for our sake (Phil. 2:7).

Quality 3: Christ was obedient. Jesus always sought to do his Father's will (Phil. 2:8, 14).

Materials

- Photocopies of the "2:14 Attitude" handout, page 137
- Pens—one for every student

Preparation

1. Read through the entire moment, familiarizing yourself with the teaching points and action steps before leading your group through the moment.
2. Photocopy the handout.

Teaching Outline

Opening

PRAY—Gather students together and open with prayer. Ask God to help students have an attitude like Jesus'. Pray that God would help the group to become a Christian community that reflects Christ's qualities.

ACTION—Distribute the pens and handouts. Ask a student to read from the handout Philippians 2:5: "Your attitude should be the same that Christ Jesus had."

TEACH—The Bible is very clear that God cares about our attitudes. The attitude we choose to have each day really does impact everything we do—from the activities we are involved in to the people we are around. Our attitudes are very important and should reflect the attitude of Jesus. In this lesson, we are going to look at three qualities in the life of Jesus that we need to model to have the right attitudes.

Quality 1: Christ was a servant.

TEACH—The first quality is Christ was a servant. As Christ-followers, we are told to have an attitude like Jesus'. The question we need to answer is: What was Jesus' attitude like? Listen to what Philippians 2:6–8 says about Jesus' attitude: "Though he was God, he did not demand and cling to his rights as God. He made himself nothing; he took the humble position of a slave and appeared in human form. And in human form he obediently humbled himself even further by dying a criminal's death on a cross."

We're going to take a few moments to talk about these verses in small groups.

ACTION—Ask students to break into groups of three or four. Give them five minutes to review Philippians 2:6–8 on the handout and discuss the Christlike qualities listed in the verses. After five minutes, call the group back together. Ask students to share their findings before proceeding.

TEACH—To get a better understanding of Christ's servant attitude, listen to Philippians 2:4: "Don't think only about your own affairs, but be interested in others, too, and what they are doing." We are to have an attitude that actively seeks out ways to serve others—an attitude that says others' interests are just as important as ours. However, this can be very difficult to do, especially in a world that says, "Take care of number one." The world says to focus on your own needs and serve only yourself. This is quite different from what Jesus asks us to do. We are to have servant attitudes toward others.

ACTION—Ask students to get back in groups of three or four and give them the following instructions:
- On your handout, look at the Servant Attitude continuum under Quality 1: Christ was a servant.
- Place an X on the continuum next to the statement that best describes your attitude about being a servant.
- Share with your group why you see yourself that way.

After three to five minutes, call the group back together.

Quality 2: Christ was humble.

TEACH—The first quality was Christ was a servant. The second quality is Christ was humble. Jesus not only had a servant attitude, he had a *humble* servant attitude. Listen to Philippians 2:7: "He made himself nothing; he took the humble position of a slave and appeared in human form." It can be very difficult to have this kind of attitude—to remain humble while the world encourages us to be prideful. That's why we need to keep our focus on Jesus and not the world. Remember, we can control our attitudes; we must stay focused on our example. Again, Christ is the example for our attitudes.

Let's talk about this in our groups.

ACTION—Ask students to get back in groups of three or four and give them the following instructions:
- On your handout, look at the Humble Attitude continuum under Quality 2: Christ was humble.
- Place an X on the continuum next to the statement that best describes your attitude about being humble.
- Share with your group why you see yourself that way.

After three to five minutes, call the group back together.

Quality 3: Christ was obedient.

TEACH—So far, we've seen that Christ was a servant and that he was humble. The third quality is Christ was obedient. This means he submitted himself to authority. Philippians 2:8 says, "And in human form he obediently humbled himself even further by dying a criminal's death on a cross." Jesus was devoted to following the direction of his heavenly Father. Following Jesus' example means being willing to do whatever God calls us to do—including submitting to authority. This can be difficult, especially when we may not respect or want to listen to authority figures, such as teachers, bosses, or even our own parents. At these times, we must remember God has asked us to have an attitude like Jesus'—one willing to submit to authority even when it's difficult. As long as the authority is not harming us or asking us to do something dishonoring to God, we need to be obedient. Remember that obedience comes out of our desire to let God be the leader and the forgiver of our lives, knowing that he loves us and has the perfect plan for our lives.

Let's talk about this in our groups.

ACTION—Ask students to get back in groups of three or four and give them the following instructions:
- On your handout, look at the Obedient Attitude continuum under Quality 3: Christ was obedient.
- Place an X on the continuum next to the statement that best describes your attitude about being obedient.
- Share with your group why you see yourself that way.

After three to five minutes, call the group back together.

TEACH—We have been talking about having an attitude like Jesus' and looking at some of the qualities of his life—that Christ was a servant, that he was humble, and that he was obedient. Philippians 2:14 describes a Christlike attitude this way: "In everything you do, stay away from complaining and arguing." This one verse sums up the kind of attitude we need to have. We could call it a "2:14 attitude." With a 2:14 attitude you do all things without grumbling or complaining. We need to challenge each other to have this kind of attitude. When we see each other leaning away from a Christlike attitude, we need to say, "You need to 2:14 it!" Hearing these words should remind us to change our attitude. That's what we need to have in our student ministry—an attitude that reflects Christ's qualities of servanthood, humility, and obedience. We all need to be willing to encourage one another by reminding each other at the right times to "2:14 it!"

At the end of your handout is the "2:14 Challenge." It says:

In the next forty-eight hours, I will:

1. Memorize Philippians 2:14.
2. Look for practical ways to be a servant to others.
3. Humble myself and consider others' interests as important as my own.
4. Keep a positive attitude toward those in authority.
5. Write "2:14" on the back of my hand and leave it there.

If you're willing to take the 2:14 challenge, there is room at the bottom of your handout to sign your name. We're going to take a few minutes individually to decide whether or not to take the challenge. If you are willing to take the challenge, sign your name on the handout and write "2:14" on the back of your hand. Take a few minutes to make your decision now.

ACTION—Give students two or three minutes to make their decisions.

Closing

TEACH—As we close our time together, I'd like those who decided to take the 2:14 challenge to stand up. It's important to see you are not alone and know there are many of us working together to have a 2:14 attitude. If you've made the commitment, please stand now.

ACTION—Give students time to stand.

TEACH—I first want to say a word to those of you who didn't stand. I want you to know that I respect you for being real with your commitment. If you have any questions after we're done here, I'd be glad to talk with you.

Now for those of you who are standing, look around. It's pretty cool to see how many have made this decision. During the next forty-eight hours, God may really surprise us with what it means to have an attitude like Christ's. If you've taken the 2:14 challenge, be sure to encourage others who have also taken the challenge. Exchange e-mails and send encouraging notes to one another. Or, if you see each other at school, hold up your fists to show the "2:14" to keep going with the Christlike attitude. It's going to be an exciting forty-eight hours for each of you! Let's close in prayer.

ACTION—Ask all students to stand.

PRAY—Ask God to help students develop a 2:14 attitude and to help them stay committed to becoming more like Christ. Thank God in advance for all he is going to teach students through this experience and how it will affect not only their lives, but also the lives of others.

Part 3

Commitment

Developing Student Ownership

Overview

In Ephesians 4, God directs us to equip the saints to do the work of ministry. The "saints" are your students. God has uniquely gifted each one and wants every student to be active in his kingdom plans. The vision moments in this section are designed to help you develop student ownership in your ministry. When students have ownership, they are committed to being active participants and not merely spectators within the ministry.

9. Between the Lines

Purpose: To challenge students to identify and defeat the obstacles that prevent them from being completely involved in serving God.

Scripture: Matthew 14:29; Matthew 14:30–31; Matthew 25:21; 1 Corinthians 12:20, 25; Philippians 4:13; Hebrews 12:1–3

10. You Matter

Purpose: To encourage students to serve by teaching them that God wants us to use our talents and strengths in community to serve him.

Scripture: Psalm 139:13–14; Matthew 25:14–30; 1 Corinthians 12:21–26

11. The Race

Purpose: To challenge students to be strong participants instead of spectators in the spiritual race God calls us to run.

Scripture: 1 Corinthians 9:24; 1 Corinthians 9:25–26; 1 Corinthians 9:27; Philippians 3:14

Assessment

Directions

Use this assessment to evaluate students' needs for teaching and training about student ownership—what it means to be committed to your ministry. For each statement, place an X on the continuum closest to the response that best describes your students. Marks on the left side of the continuum indicate students would benefit from a vision moment in that area.

Most students have decided to . . . Between the Lines

(Go to page 63.)

Let themselves be sidelined by obstacles	Wait until it gets easier to serve God	Take some initial steps to serve God	Actively work to overcome obstacles to serve God	Do whatever it takes to serve God more fully

Most students feel they . . . You Matter

(Go to page 72.)

Have nothing to offer	Have some talents but don't see how they would be helpful	Have talents and strengths but are unsure how to use them	Have valuable talents and strengths and use them occasionally	Are working together with others to use their talents and strengths

Most students have chosen to . . . The Race

(Go to page 79.)

Be spectators in our ministry	Only rarely get involved in ministry activities	Periodically engage in ministry activities	Be committed to making our ministry work	Consistently own and help others to engage in the ministry

VISION MOMENT 9

BETWEEN THE LINES

Purpose

To challenge students to identify and defeat the obstacles that prevent them from being completely involved in serving God.

Overview

This vision moment takes place on a football field. Students are challenged to stay between the lines (BTL)—an expression used by athletes to say they want to be on the playing field, not on the bench or sidelines. Starting in one end zone, students are led down the field to the opposite end zone. During this "journey" they face the fears and obstacles that could be preventing them from staying BTL in their service to God and in their ministry as a team.

Through prayer and teamwork, we can all be BTL for God by making four decisions:

Decision 1: Step onto the playing field. To build the Kingdom, God wants us to be participants not spectators (Matt. 14:29).

Decision 2: Face your fears and doubts. We need to keep our eyes on Jesus so he can give us strength to overcome our fears and doubts (Matt. 14:30–31; Phil. 4:13).

Decision 3: Play for an audience of one. We need to focus on God's approval, not the world's approval (Heb. 12:1–3).

Decision 4: Be a team player. We can do more together than we could ever do alone (1 Cor. 12:20, 25).

Materials

- One Bible
- Poster board and paint
- Butcher paper
- Duct tape
- Six track hurdles

Preparation

1. Read through the entire moment, familiarizing yourself with the teaching points and action steps before leading your group through the moment.
2. Secure permission to use a high school football field. (Note: This moment has a greater impact when done at night with the field lights on.) If possible, also secure permission to use the public address (PA) system so you can announce each student's name as he or she steps on the field.
3. Prepare a list naming every student who will be at the event.
4. Wrap butcher paper around six track hurdles. Paint the following words in large letters on the butcher paper:
   - Hurdle 1: Pride
   - Hurdle 2: Fear (In smaller letters, you may also want to write a few examples, such as *rejection, failure,* and *future,* etc.)
   - Hurdle 3: Busyness
   - Hurdle 4: Complacency
   - Hurdle 5: Sin
   - Hurdle 6: Doubts
5. Starting from the end zone, place hurdles 1 and 2 on the hash marks of the ten-yard line. Place hurdles 3 and 4 on the hash marks of the thirty-yard line. Place hurdles 5 and 6 on the hash marks of the fifty-yard line.
6. Use the butcher paper to make a big banner (like the ones you see the players run through at football games). On the banner, paint the names of the schools your students attend. Hang the banner between the goalposts in the opposite end zone. If you are not able to make a big

banner, paint the school names on poster boards and tape them to the goalposts. See the diagram on page 138 to help you set up.

Teaching Outline

Opening

PRAY—Gather students together along the sideline of the football field and open with prayer. Ask God to give students a clear picture of what it means to be on the playing field for him. Pray that God would help students see themselves as a team that can work together to win the spiritual battle he has called us all to fight.

TEACH—BTL stands for "between the lines." It's an expression used by athletes to say they want to be on the playing field, not on the bench or sidelines. God calls each of us to be BTL —to be on the playing field with him.

ACTION—Read Matthew 14:29: "'All right, come,' Jesus said. So Peter went over the side of the boat and walked on the water toward Jesus."

Decision 1: Step onto the playing field.

TEACH—The first decision you need to make to be BTL for God is step onto the playing field. The verse we just read is from a story about Peter, who was with the other disciples in a boat when they got caught in a strong storm. Although Jesus knew Peter was frightened, Jesus invited Peter to step out of the boat and onto the water.

Jesus wants to issue the same invitation to you. Are you willing to accept it? Jesus is asking you, in a sense, to get out of the boat—to get off the sidelines and onto the playing field—to be BTL for him. It's time to make your first decision: Are you ready to step onto the playing field? If so, when your name is called, walk from the sidelines to the end zone and wait there for the next decision.

ACTION—Read students' names out loud one at a time and direct them to walk to the end zone—the one without the banner or posters—and wait there. If you have access to a PA system, an assistant can use it to announce the names just as an announcer names the starting lineup before a football game.

TEACH—Congratulations on making your first decision to make a difference for God by stepping off the sidelines and onto the playing field to be BTL for him. Now that we're on the playing field, what's next? What does God want us to do? God wants us to work together as a team to be difference-makers in his kingdom. Our goal is to get to the end zone and to score spiritually for God, helping others to know God's love, staying faithful and committed to his plan for our lives. It's a long way and it's going to take teamwork to get there, but it's worth it. There are obstacles trying to keep us from getting to the end zone. These obstacles are trying to disqualify us and keep us from staying BTL. That leads us to the next decision.

Decision 2: Face your fears and doubts.

TEACH—The second decision you need to make to be BTL for God is face your fears and doubts. That's what Peter had to do.

ACTION—Read Matthew 14:30–31: "But when he looked around at the high waves, he was terrified and began to sink. 'Save me, Lord!' he shouted. Instantly Jesus reached out his hand and grabbed him. 'You don't have much faith,' Jesus said. 'Why did you doubt me?'"

TEACH—Here we pick up the story after Peter stepped out of the boat. Peter was fine until he took his eyes off Jesus. When he started to focus on the storm, he became frightened and fearful he wouldn't make it. This is exactly what keeps many of us from staying BTL for God—we start to doubt we can make it. We become afraid. We lose our focus, take our eyes off Jesus, and start to be consumed by our fears instead. Fortunately, Christ is stronger than our fears.

ACTION—Read Philippians 4:13: "For I can do everything with the help of Christ who gives me the strength I need."

TEACH—We must be willing to go down the field and face the obstacles and fears that keep us from staying BTL for God, knowing he will help us. Directly in front of us on the ten-yard line are two hurdles. On each hurdle is an obstacle we might face as we strive to serve and follow God. In just a moment, I'll ask you to stand behind the hurdle that best describes your obstacles. The first obstacles that you'll be facing are fear and pride—fear of giving God complete control of your life or making a stand for what you believe or pride that keeps you from staying humble and admitting when you are wrong. Remember that we can do all things through Christ who gives us strength. We can overcome these obstacles by asking for God's help through prayer. It's time to make the decision to face your doubts and fears.

> **ACTION**—Give students the following instructions:
> - Stand behind the hurdle that represents an obstacle—pride or fear—you need to face. (twenty-yard line)
> - Take a moment to pray silently. Ask God to help you overcome this obstacle.
>
> After a few minutes, pray out loud for the students. Ask God to help them overcome these obstacles and stay BTL for him.
> Ask the first student in line behind each hurdle to knock it down and walk over it. Invite the other students to follow and continue walking down the field to the twenty-yard line.

TEACH—It feels good to be on a team moving together in the same direction for God. We can do much more together than we could ever do alone. There is still a long way to go, and the enemy wants to stop us from staying BTL. He wants to knock us off the field, but if we stay together we can win for God. Now that we've gotten through the first obstacle, we see there are still more to face: busyness and complacency. Busyness keeps us from spending time with God and encourages us to fill our lives so full that we neglect time with God. Complacency stops us from giving our best to God, getting involved, and using our spiritual gifts to make a difference for him.

> **ACTION**—Give students the following instructions:

- Stand behind the hurdle that represents an obstacle—busy-ness or complacency—you need to face. (thirty-yard line)
- Take a moment to pray silently. Ask God to help you over-come this obstacle.

After a few minutes, pray out loud for the students. Ask God to help them overcome these obstacles and stay BTL for him.

Ask the first student in line behind each hurdle to knock it down and walk over it. Invite the other students to follow and continue walk-ing down the field to the forty-yard line.

TEACH—We are making progress and becoming stronger as a team. But we still have some hurdles to tackle. We must continue to face them together. The next obstacles are sin and doubt. Sins are things we know are dishonoring to God—habits, activities, relation-ships—things we know we need to stop or change in order to honor God. Doubt is like an internal voice that tells us that we aren't good enough, or that we have nothing to offer to God. Doubts mislead us into believing we can't change or make a difference for God.

ACTION—Give students the following instructions:
- Stand behind the hurdle that represents an obstacle—sin or doubt—you need to face. (fifty-yard line)
- Take a moment to pray silently. Ask God to help you over-come this obstacle.

After a few minutes, pray out loud for the students. Ask God to help them overcome these obstacles and stay BTL for him.

Ask the first student in line behind each hurdle to knock it down and walk over it. Invite the other students to follow and continue walk-ing down the field to the forty-yard line. (You are now on the oppo-nent's side of the field.)

Decision 3: Play for an audience of one.

TEACH—We have made good progress! We are now on the opponent's forty-yard line—we are now on the opponent's side of the playing field. The enemy still wants to stop us from staying BTL, so we need to keep our focus on God. We must now make our third decision, which is to play for an audience of one. Athletes like to hear an audience cheer and applaud—it encourages them to keep going. When we're BTL for God, we may not hear a lot of cheering or encouraging words—especially here in the enemy's territory. Taking a stand for God can be difficult at times. Choosing to do the right thing may make us feel very alone. At these times it's important to remember that the Bible says we are not alone. These stands may be empty today, but there are stands that are filled in heaven with men and women of the faith who have gone before us and are encouraging us to keep faithful and playing for God's approval, not the world's approval. Listen to these words.

ACTION—Read Hebrews 12:1–3: "Therefore, since we are surrounded by such a huge crowd of witnesses to the life of faith, let us strip off every weight that slows us down, especially the sin that so easily hinders our progress. And let us run with endurance the race that God has set before us. We do this by keeping our eyes on Jesus, on whom our faith depends from start to finish. He was willing to die a shameful death on the cross because of the joy he knew would be his afterward. Now he is seated in the place of highest honor beside God's throne in heaven. Think about all he endured when sinful people did such terrible things to him, so that you don't become weary and give up."

TEACH—These verses remind us there is a huge crowd of Christians—witnesses of the faith—cheering us on. These are the countless men and women who have served God in the past and are now cheering us on to stay BTL—encouraging us to keep moving down the field to make a difference for God. These "cheerleaders" remind us to play for an audience of one—for God. That is our motivation, to know that someday we'll stand before God and he will say, "Well done, my good and faithful child" (Matt. 25:21).

ACTION—Invite students to line up alongside each other on the forty-yard line. Stand in front of them on the thirty-yard line.

TEACH—Now it's time to make the third decision: Are you willing to play for an audience of one? Even when it gets difficult and you feel all alone, when you see no one around to cheer you on, you need to remain faithful. You need to be willing to take a stand, play for an audience of one, and stay BTL for God. If you are ready to make this decision, walk quietly down to the twenty-yard line. As you walk, remember the huge crowd of heavenly saints that are cheering you on to the finish line.

ACTION—Direct students to walk quietly to the opponent's twenty-yard line.

Decision 4: Be a team player.

TEACH—We are very close to our goal. We had to make several decisions to get this far. Now there is only one decision left: Be a team player. We find ourselves in what is called the "red zone." It gets tough down here because we are very close to scoring. This is when the battle is at its most intense. It's also where we have to pull together as a team because the stakes are extremely high. The end zone represents our schools and our friends who don't know Christ. That's what the game is all about, that's what we are fighting for, and that's why we must be a team together. We want to build a team that can really make a difference in every school in our community. We must work together to make a difference and to fulfill God's plans for us—individually and as a student ministry.

ACTION—Read I Corinthians 12:20 and 25: "Yes, there are many parts, but only one body. . . . This makes for harmony among the members, so that all the members care for each other equally."

TEACH—What we just read is a reminder that every person is important. Every person has his or her own spiritual gift, and when we all use our gifts together to reach the common goal, we become the body of Christ. When we build a community with each other, we can score spiritually together, knowing everyone is important and needed. If you are ready to make this fourth and final decision to be a team player, then take the hand of the person next to you. By taking his or her hand, you're saying, "I want to be BTL as a team."

ACTION—Invite students on the twenty-yard line to join hands and walk together into the end zone. Once in the end zone, gather students together and huddle up for closing words and a final prayer.

Closing

TEACH—I'm proud of each of you for your decision to be BTL for God, for your courage to face the obstacles that could put you back on the sidelines and out of the action God wants you to be a part of. I'm thankful for your desire to be a team, a community—to make a difference together in the lives of many of your friends in your schools. You are all players for God's kingdom.

PRAY—Thank God for bringing these students together to be players for the kingdom and to be BTL as a team for him. Ask God to help students overcome their obstacles and stay tough on the playing field of faith so their family and friends can be impacted by their commitment to be BTL.

VISION MOMENT 10

YOU MATTER

Purpose

To encourage students to serve by teaching them that God wants us to use our talents and strengths in community to serve him.

Overview

This vision moment takes place indoors. Students are given the opportunity to reflect on the contribution they make in the ministry. Using pieces of a homemade jigsaw puzzle to represent their unique God-given talents, students add their piece to the puzzle as a symbol of their decision to contribute to the ministry by using their talents.

We can see a clear picture of how God intends for us to serve him by looking at three timeless truths about service.

Truth 1: We have each been given unique strengths. God created us uniquely and we can all play a key part in his plan to reach those who are not yet Christ-followers (Ps. 139:13–14).

Truth 2: We need each other. We can't accomplish everything on our own; we are dependent on each others' strengths (1 Cor. 12:21–26).

Truth 3: We must choose to contribute our part. God desires for us to make a decision to get involved, to invest what he has given us to make a difference for his kingdom (Matt. 25:14–30).

Materials

- Bibles
- Photocopies of the "You Matter" handout, page 139

- Two three-by-two-foot white poster boards
- Broad-tip permanent marker
- Fine-tip permanent markers—one for every student
- Pencil
- Scissors
- Medium-size cardboard box

Preparation

1. Read through the entire moment, familiarizing yourself with the teaching points and action steps before leading your group through the moment.
2. With a broad-tip permanent marker, write your ministry's mission statement on both poster boards. Write large enough so the entire surface area is utilized. If you don't have a mission statement, write your ministry's name or the following Bible verse: "Love the Lord your God with all your heart, all your soul, all your mind, and all your strength" (Mark 12:30).
3. Using a pencil, lightly draw interlocking puzzle pieces on one poster board so there are enough pieces for each student, plus five extra pieces. The pieces should be large enough to allow students to write clearly on the blank side. Each puzzle piece should have a part of the mission statement showing on it to facilitate putting the puzzle back together.
4. Cut along the pencil lines to create individual puzzle pieces.
5. Place the puzzle pieces in the cardboard box to make them easy to carry and pass among students.
6. Photocopy the handout.

Teaching Outline

Opening

PRAY—Gather students together in a semicircle facing you—the uncut poster board with the mission statement should be visible behind you so that your students clearly see the mission of your ministry. Open with prayer. Ask God to help the students fully understand how each one is a masterpiece of his handiwork— marvelously unique—and how each one has a part to play in God's overall plan.

TEACH—Each one of you has a unique contribution to make to the success of this team. A healthy ministry requires a combination of people who like to create things, handle details, greet people, lead worship, perform dramas, take care of others, provide vision, lead, shepherd, teach, and more. An effective ministry involves gifted people bringing their talents and strengths together for the common purpose of spreading God's message of hope. We can put together a clearer picture of what this looks like by looking at three truths of serving.

Truth 1: We have each been given unique strengths.

TEACH—Truth 1 is we have each been given unique strengths. Listen to Psalm 139:13–14: "You made all the delicate, inner parts of my body and knit them together in my mother's womb. Thank you for making me so wonderfully complex! Your workmanship is mar- velous—and how well I know that."

When God created you, he made you unique. By God's design, each one of us is different—with a combination of abilities and skills unlike anyone else's. We all have something unique to contribute.

ACTION—Pass around the box containing the puzzle pieces and ask each student to take a piece. Put the box with the extra pieces off to the side—you'll use them later.

Distribute the handouts.

TEACH—We all have God-given strengths and abilities. That's what these puzzle pieces represent—the things you are good at or that just come naturally to you. Whatever your talents and gifts, God has given them to you for a specific purpose. He has plans for how you can use your strengths to help others understand more about him.

ACTION—Using the handout as a guide, give some examples of strengths you see in your students. Give students the following instructions:

- Take a moment to review the list of strengths and abilities on your handout. Circle any statements that describe gifts or talents you think you might have.
- Complete the statement, "I believe my top two strengths are . . . ," by writing your strengths in the space provided on the handout.
- On the back of your puzzle piece, write your top two strengths and this statement: "I can use my strengths in our ministry by . . ." Complete the statement by listing two or three ways you can contribute to the ministry. If you're unsure, just make your best guess.
- You have about five minutes.

After about five minutes (when you see most students are done), give students the following instructions:

- Gather in groups of three or four.
- Share with each other the two strengths you identified and how you think you might use your strengths to contribute to our ministry.
- You have about ten minutes.

After about ten minutes, gather the group back together.

Truth 2: We need each other.

ACTION—Ask a student to read I Corinthians 12:21–26: "The eye can never say to the hand, 'I don't need you.' The head can't say to the feet, 'I don't need you.' In fact, some of the parts that seem weakest and least important are really the most necessary. And the parts we regard as less honorable are those we clothe with the greatest care. So we carefully protect from the eyes of others those parts that should not be seen, while other parts do not require this special care. So God has put the body together in such a way that extra honor and care are given to those parts that have less dignity. This makes for harmony among the members, so that all the members care for each other equally. If one part suffers, all the parts suffer with it, and if one part is honored, all the parts are glad."

TEACH—The Bible tells us that we need each other. That is Truth 2. God created us in his image, which in part means we have a desire to be in community with him and with one another. He created us with unique strengths and talents so we would need to depend upon each other—nobody can do it all, and we weren't intended to go it alone. We can each become a key part of this ministry community, but we need each other to effectively reach others who are not Christ-followers.

ACTION—Give students the following instructions:
- Gather again in groups of three or four.
- One at a time, name your strengths and gifts. As a group, discuss together how that person's gifts could be used in our ministry and why that person's gifts are important. Focus on one person at a time until you've discussed everyone in your group.

Every two or three minutes, alert students to move on to discussing the next person in the group so every student has a chance to share his or her gifts. When you see that most small groups are done, call students back together and ask them to sit in a circle.

Truth 3: We must choose to contribute our part.

TEACH—Truth 3 is we must choose to contribute our part. We need to take ownership of the unique contribution we can make. We need to step up and be willing to use the talents and strengths God has given us—that's why he gave them to us in the first place. It all comes down to the individual decisions we make on a daily basis to contribute what we can and be all that God has made us to be.

ACTION—Ask everyone to turn in their Bibles to Matthew 25:14–30. Ask one student to read the story of the three servants aloud while everyone else follows along.

TEACH—This parable shows how God wants us to serve him— by doing the best we can with what he has given us. Every day we need to choose to use our talents and strengths for God's kingdom and not bury or waste them.

ACTION—Ask students to assemble the puzzle by having each person put in his or her own puzzle piece. It is important that everyone put in only one piece to symbolize an individual willingness to make a contribution to the ministry. Students will eventually notice that some pieces are missing; tell them to assemble the puzzle as best they can.

TEACH—Some puzzle pieces are missing. The missing pieces represent people who are not yet a part of our ministry. They might be friends, teammates, or classmates who need to be invited to join our community. Who do you know who might enjoy contributing their unique talents to our ministry?

ACTION—Retrieve the box with the remaining puzzle pieces. Give students the box with the following instructions:
- Think about people you know. Are there friends you would like to invite to join our ministry team? If so, write their names on the back of a puzzle piece.
- Think about our ministry. Are there any positions that need to be filled? If so, write those positions on the back of a puzzle piece.
- If you can't think of a person to invite or a position to fill, write a question mark on a puzzle piece to represent the unknown people God may bring to our ministry.
- Once you're done writing, use the pieces to complete the puzzle.

When the puzzle is complete, students should be able to read the ministry's mission statement written there.

TEACH—We need to realize that only when everyone contributes their part will we ever be able to accomplish what is written here. We are incomplete when we are missing someone's part, and our whole ministry team suffers. On a daily basis we need to be committed to contribute our part, and we need to consistently encourage others to do the same. We have amazing potential to make a difference for the Kingdom if we simply commit to do together what we could never accomplish alone.

Closing

ACTION—Invite students to take their puzzle pieces out of the puzzle. Encourage them to put their pieces someplace where they will see them often and be reminded of the unique contribution they can choose to make to the ministry.

TEACH—It's amazing that God has given each one of us unique talents and strengths, and it is awesome to see what he can do with us together as a ministry if we each choose to serve him daily.

PRAY—Thank God for loving us so much that he created each one of us uniquely. Ask him to continue to show students what talents and strengths he has given to them. Also ask him to help students make the daily decision to give their best effort to serve him and to work together as a community to follow him more fully.

VISION MOMENT 11

THE RACE

Purpose

To challenge students to be strong participants instead of spectators in the spiritual race God calls us to run.

Overview

This vision moment takes place outdoors at a park or school where students can sit in the bleachers in front of a running track. Students are challenged to be ministry participants rather than ministry spectators. They make their decision public by stepping out of the bleachers and onto the track. They walk one lap around the track, quietly reflecting on three objectives of running the spiritual race.

We can become strong participants in the spiritual race God has called us to run by remembering three objectives.

Objective 1: Run to win the prize. We need to give our best as we pursue an authentic relationship with Christ (1 Cor. 9:24).

Objective 2: Run with purpose. We do not run aimlessly. We run to help God build his kingdom (1 Cor. 9:25–26).

Objective 3: Run without being disqualified. We must stay focused on the goal of winning the race and not be distracted by things that would take us off course spiritually (1 Cor. 9:27).

Materials

- Bibles

Preparation

1. Read through the entire moment, familiarizing yourself with the teaching points and action steps before leading your group through the moment.
2. At least one week ahead, secure permission to use a park or school where there are bleachers and a track.
3. Ask a volunteer to go to the park or school ahead of time to make sure no one is sitting in the bleachers.

Teaching Outline

Opening

PRAY—Gather students together and open in prayer. Thank God for allowing students the opportunity to be involved with advancing his kingdom. Ask God to help students move from being ministry spectators to ministry participants in this Kingdom work.

ACTION—Ask students to sit in the bleachers. Stand on the ground facing them as you teach.

TEACH—Right now you're sitting in the bleachers where spectators usually sit. Let me ask you a couple questions:
1. What is the difference between a spectator and a participant?
2. What does a spectator miss?

ACTION—Possible responses:
- A spectator watches, but participants get fully involved in the event.
- A spectator never really knows what it's like to be involved; a participant knows exactly what it's like to be involved.
- Participants feel victories and defeats more strongly than spectators.

Ask one or two students to read the following verses: "Remember that in a race everyone runs, but only one person gets the prize. You also must run in such a way that you will win" (1 Cor. 9:24).

"I strain to reach the end of the race and receive the prize for which God, through Christ Jesus, is calling us up to heaven" (Phil. 3:14).

Objective 1: Run to win the prize.

TEACH—The reason you are sitting in the bleachers is to remind you that God has called every one of us to be participants, not spectators. We are here at the track as a reminder that God calls all Christians to run in a spiritual race—a race to help God build his kingdom. The Bible tells us that our first objective in this race is run to win the prize. God wants us to give our best—to have an attitude that says, "I'm not just in the spiritual race to run. I'm in the spiritual race to win!" As we begin to run this spiritual race, we need to ask ourselves two questions:

1. What is the purpose of the race?
2. What is the prize we are running for?

Trying to answer these questions leads us to the second objective.

Objective 2: Run with purpose.

ACTION—Ask a student to read I Corinthians 9:25–26: "All athletes practice strict self-control. They do it to win a prize that will fade away, but we do it for an eternal prize. So I run straight to the goal with purpose in every step. I am not like a boxer who misses his punches."

TEACH—Our second objective in running the race is run with purpose. Because the goal we are pursuing is helping God build his kingdom, God does not want us to run aimlessly—he calls us to run toward this goal with great determination. So this answers our first question of what the purpose of the race is—the purpose is to advance God's kingdom. We do not run for prizes of the world—money, fame, and success—that will someday be gone. We run for a prize that will last forever—an eternal crown. This answers our second question about what the prize we are running for is. God calls each of us to run with intense purpose as we help him build his kingdom and earn an eternal prize far greater than anything the world can offer. The race God calls us to run is like no other.

The apostle Paul understood the importance of this race. That's why he said in 1 Corinthians 9:19, "This means I am not bound to obey people just because they pay me, yet I have become a servant of everyone so that I can bring them to Christ." What do you think Paul was talking about in this verse?

ACTION—Allow several students to respond before proceeding. Possible responses:

- He is not doing it as a job to earn money, but out of his love and calling to follow Jesus.
- He is motivated out of his love for others, to see them become Christ-followers.
- He is not concerned about what people think but about what God has called him to.

TEACH—Paul was talking about the importance of telling people about God—about helping people understand God's love for them. As we run the race with great purpose to help God build his kingdom, we want others to come to know God and join us in the race. That's why this next objective is so important.

Objective 3: Run without being disqualified.

ACTION—Ask a student to read 1 Corinthians 9:27: "I discipline my body like an athlete, training it to do what it should. Otherwise, I fear that after preaching to others I myself might be disqualified."

TEACH—The third objective we must remember is run without being disqualified. The race God calls us to run will cost us something. Just like any athlete who trains to participate in an event, we must prepare ourselves and stay focused on our goal. We must also know what would disqualify us from the event. The Bible talks about an enemy who is constantly trying to disqualify us from the race—to tempt us to walk away from what God has called us to, to take ourselves out of the race by becoming spectators rather than participants. Can you name some ways the enemy might try to disqualify us?

ACTION—Allow several students to respond before proceeding. Possible responses:
- To urge us to give in to the temptation to sin
- To listen to the lies that tell us we cannot be used by God
- To make us feel guilty and not accept God's forgiveness and grace

TEACH—We cannot let the enemy disqualify us—we must stay focused on the objectives of the race: serving God and building his kingdom. Our challenge is to think about the spiritual race God has called us to run and make a decision to be participants rather than spectators. As participants, we need to help each other stay focused on the three objectives of the race:
- Run to win.
- Run with purpose.
- Run without being disqualified.

In just a moment, you are going to have an opportunity to give a public demonstration of your decision to run the race by stepping out of the bleachers and stepping onto the track. By doing this, you are saying you are no longer going to be a spectator, but you're going to be a participant by running God's race. You're going to find out the role you can play in helping God build his kingdom by loving him and loving others.

PRAY—Ask God to give each student the courage to enter the race he has called them to—to no longer be a spectator but a strong participant in making a difference for his kingdom.

TEACH—If you're ready to become a participant, then stand up now and join me on the track.

ACTION—Give students time to step onto the track.

TEACH—I am very excited about the decision each of you has made. I know God has great plans for you in the race he's called you to. To mark this moment, we're going to quietly walk one lap around the track on our own. As you walk, think about the three objectives.

- First, we run to win. Ask God to give you the determination to win the race he's called you to.
- Second, we run with purpose. Think about a friend you can share Christ with, a friend you'd love to have in the race with you.
- Third, we run without being disqualified. Ask God to give you accountability and determination to stay in the race. Some of you may need to ask for God's forgiveness for where you already feel disqualified from the race and accept his grace to get back into the race he's called you to. Others of you need to ask God for strength to not give in to temptation or listen to the enemy's lies but to stay focused on God's truth. Ask God for perseverance and determination to finish the race strong.

Once you take your lap, we'll meet back here and close in prayer.

ACTION—Send students off to walk around the track. Be sensitive to any students still in the stands who did not make this decision. Invite them to join the others in walking around the track. Ask them to think about what is preventing them from joining in the race God has called them to.

After all students have taken a lap around the track, bring them together and close in prayer.

Closing

PRAY—Thank God for the race he has called students to run and for giving them the strength they will need along the way. Ask him to help students run this race to win, to run with purpose, and not to disqualify themselves so they can be victorious with God's help.

Part 4

Evangelism
A Heart for Others

Overview

In Matthew 9:37, Jesus makes it clear that the harvest is indeed plentiful, but the workers are few. We need to do all we can to prepare this generation to go out into the harvest fields. One of today's greatest harvests is this young generation. The vision moments in this section encourage, motivate, and challenge students to be the workers for their generation—to win one life at a time with the love of Christ.

12. Called to Contribute

Purpose: To instill a sense of urgency in students by helping them understand we have limited time to bring others into a relationship with Christ.

Scripture: Matthew 22:36–40; Matthew 28:19–20; John 11:25; Romans 10:9; Romans 10:14–15; James 4:14

13. Vision Walk

Purpose: To motivate and challenge students to make a difference in the spiritual condition of their schools.

Scripture: Nehemiah 1–2; Nehemiah 1:11; Nehemiah 2:11–13; Nehemiah 2:17; Nehemiah 2:18

14. One Life at a Time

Purpose: To challenge every student to share Christ with one friend during the school year.

Scripture: Matthew 21:22; John 9:25; Acts 2:42–43

For Additional Training

After experiencing an evangelism vision moment, your students may be motivated to take the next steps in relational evangelism. The *Becoming a Contagious Christian, Youth Edition* curriculum is a great evangelism training resource for equipping students to share Christ. For more information about *Becoming a Contagious Christian, Youth Edition* and other student ministry resources, visit www.WCAstudentministries.com.

Assessment

Directions

Use this assessment to evaluate students' needs for teaching and training in evangelism. For each statement, place an *X* on the continuum closest to the response that best describes your students. Marks on the left side of the continuum suggest students would benefit from a vision moment in that area.

Students feel . . .   **Called to Contribute**
(Go to page 87.)

Nothing—they rarely think about sharing Christ	It's no big deal—they feel they're young and have plenty of time	Concerned sometimes that their friends are not Christians	Life is short; they want to do all they can to reach their non-Christian friends	Excited that God wants to use them to reach their non-Christian friends this year

Students believe . . .   **Vision Walk**
(Go to page 93.)

No one at their school cares about God—what's the use in sharing their faith?	There is no spiritual purpose for why they are at their school	God could really change their school to honor himself	God can use them to make an eternal difference at their school	God has placed them at their school for a reason—and it's to be a minister to their campus

Students believe God can . . .   **One Life at a Time**
(Go to page 100.)

Change lives in general but not their friends'	Use other people but not them	Use them someday but not now	Use them to talk about Christ with their friends	Use them to lead their friends to Christ this year

CALLED TO CONTRIBUTE

Purpose

To instill a sense of urgency in students by helping them understand they have limited time to bring others into a relationship with Christ.

Overview

This vision moment takes place in a cemetery. Students walk through the cemetery to help them reflect on the inevitability of physical death and to give them a sense of urgency about sharing Christ with friends who don't yet have a personal relationship with him.

Students should be enthusiastically committed to bringing their friends into a relationship with Christ because of three biblical truths.

> *Truth 1: Physical death is certain.* Life is brief and physical death is inevitable (James 4:14).

> *Truth 2: Eternal life is available to everyone.* It is God's free gift of salvation for all who will accept it (John 11:25; Rom. 10:9).

> *Truth 3: God asks us to be involved in bringing people to him.* As Christians, we have a responsibility to spread Christ's message of hope (Matt. 28:19–20; Rom. 10:14–15).

Materials

- Bibles
- Photocopies of the "Called to Contribute" handout, page 140

Preparation

1. Read through the entire moment, familiarizing yourself with the teaching points and action steps before leading your group through the moment.
2. At least one week ahead, contact a cemetery and secure permission to walk around the grounds and spend time talking there.
3. Photocopy the handout.

Teaching Outline

Opening

PRAY—Gather students together in a quiet area of the cemetery and open with prayer. Ask God to give everyone an eternal perspective on the biblical truths about life and death.

TEACH—We're here today to get a clear understanding of the biblical truths about life and death and to discuss the part we each play in helping our friends come to know God. To do this, we're going to consider three biblical truths.

Truth 1: Physical death is certain.

TEACH—The first truth is physical death is certain. As we look around the cemetery, it's pretty obvious that death is inevitable. We may not know when we are going to die, but it is certain that we will.

ACTION—Ask a student to read James 4:14 (NIV): "You are a mist that appears for a little while and then vanishes."
Option: Use a spray bottle filled with water to visually demonstrate how quickly a mist disappears—that it is here for a second and then gone.

TEACH—When we fully grasp how brief our physical lives really are, it can make us think about what happens after we die. We're going to take some time now to walk around the cemetery so we can reflect on the truth of James 4:14.

ACTION—Give students the following instructions:

- Walk around the cemetery and look at the grave markers. Read the names, the birth and death dates, and anything else written about the deceased.
- Pay attention to your thoughts and feelings. We'll talk about your observations when we get back together.
- While you are walking in silence, prayerfully ask God to help you understand more fully the deeper truths about life and death.
- You'll have ten minutes to take your walks and then we'll meet back here.

After ten minutes, gather the group back together. Help students process their experiences by asking them to share their observations, thoughts, and feelings with the group. Ask:

- As you walked around, what was it that got your attention?
- What did it make you think of or feel and why?

Possible responses:

- It made me sad to see a grave marker with the same first/last name as mine on it.
- I was completely surprised to see a grave of someone that was born the same year as me.
- I felt very sad because of a loss of someone close to me. I just wanted it to be over.
- I don't like to think of the reality of death; it makes me uncomfortable.

Truth 2: Eternal life is available to everyone.

TEACH—The second truth is eternal life is available to everyone. Even though physical death is certain, eternal life is available to everyone who accepts the gift God has given us in his Son, Jesus Christ.

ACTION—Ask one or two students to read the following verses: "For if you confess with your mouth that Jesus is Lord and believe in your heart that God raised him from the dead, you will be saved" (Rom. 10:9). "'I am the resurrection and the life. Those who believe in me, even though they die like everyone else, will live again'" (John 11:25).

TEACH—These are amazing words. God has the power to transform lives. He offers each of us life beyond death—eternity with him!

ACTION—Ask students the following questions, one at a time:
- How does it change your perspective on life and death, knowing you have received God's gift of eternal life?
- Do you know anyone who has not yet accepted God's gift of eternal life? (Encourage students to share names with the group.)

Truth 3: God asks us to be involved in bringing people to him.

TEACH—The third truth is God asks us to be involved in bringing people to him. He wants our help to spread the good news about his gift of eternal life. There is a part all of us can play in reaching our friends who don't yet know him. The greatest commandment is to love God and to love others (Matt. 22:36–40). The greatest act of love we can offer another person is to introduce him or her to Jesus.

ACTION—Ask a student to read Romans 10:14–15: "But how can they call on him to save unless they believe in him? And how can they believe in him if they have never heard about him? And how can they hear about him unless somebody tells them? And how will anyone go and tell them without being sent? That is what the Scriptures mean when they say, 'How beautiful are the feet of those who bring good news!'"

TEACH—These verses make it clear that we need to tell our friends about Jesus. We can do this in a couple of ways. In addition to telling our friends about God's love, we can also demonstrate God's love by helping out with a need they have. When we consistently demonstrate an attitude of service, it makes our friends want to know what motivates us to do these things. This then creates an opening for us to share the relationship we have with Christ.

ACTION—Ask a student to read Matthew 28:19–20: "'Therefore, go and make disciples of all the nations, baptizing them in the name of the Father and the Son and the Holy Spirit. Teach these new disciples to obey all the commands I have given you. And be sure of this: I am with you always, even to the end of the age.'"

TEACH—Jesus told his disciples to be his witnesses to all nations. We are his disciples today, and his plan has not changed— we still have the same mandate to deliver Christ's message of love and hope. Each one of us is called to build the church by sharing Christ with our friends who don't yet know him.

God's design is for us to work together to tell others about Christ. He intends for us to deliver this message of love and forgiveness by working together, using the unique gifts he has given each one of us. Isn't it reassuring to know we don't have to do this by ourselves? In addition to the support we get from each other, we also have the confidence of knowing the Holy Spirit is working within us. That is powerful and encouraging!

ACTION—Ask students to partner with one other person and give them seven to ten minutes to discuss the following questions from the handout:
- What would it mean for you to take an active role in telling your friends about Christ?
- What is holding you back from telling your friends about Christ?
- What first step can you take to share Christ with your friends?

After seven to ten minutes, call the group back together. Before proceeding, ask a few students to share the first steps they plan to take to share Christ with their friends.

Closing

TEACH—Listen again to Jesus' words from Matthew 28: "Therefore, go and make disciples of all the nations, baptizing them in the name of the Father and the Son and the Holy Spirit. Teach these new disciples to obey all the commands I have given you. And be sure of this: I am with you always, even to the end of the age."

What would it look like if our ministry lived out these words every day? What would it mean to our friends? Can you imagine the strength of going out together to reach our friends and family for Jesus? Can you imagine that friend or family member you mentioned earlier getting to know Jesus personally? Can you imagine the excitement and anticipation around what God can do? It can happen and God can use us. We just need to be committed to doing our part. Before you go to sleep tonight, thank God for the gift of eternal life and ask him to give you courage and guidance to become actively involved in his plan to tell your friends about Christ.

PRAY—Thank God for his amazing gift of eternal life with him. Thank him for the people in our lives who don't yet know him. Ask God to give students the courage to actively reach out to their friends and share the eternal, life-changing good news of Jesus Christ.

VISION MOMENT 13

VISION WALK

Purpose

To motivate and challenge students to make a difference in the spiritual condition of their schools.

Overview

This moment takes place on a junior high or high school campus. Students take a "vision walk"—a private walk around the school—to pray and ask God to help them to see their school the way he sees it. They ask God to give them opportunities to tell their friends how God has changed their lives and to use them to help their friends learn about God.

Every student can make a difference on his or her campus by taking a personal vision walk and making three prayer requests:

Prayer Request 1: God, help me to see my school the way you see it. God wants to use us to impact the spiritual condition of our schools (Neh. 2:11–13).

Prayer Request 2: God, give me opportunities to share my story with one of my non-Christian friends. God wants to use our stories to share his love with others (Neh. 2:18).

Prayer Request 3: God, give me success in helping my friends become Christians and give me the approval of those in authority at my school. God can make us effective and give us favor with those in authority (Neh. 1:11).

Materials

- Bibles
- Photocopies of the "Vision Walk" handout, page 141
- Pens/pencils—one for every student

Preparation

1. Read through the entire moment, familiarizing yourself with the teaching points and action steps before leading your group through the moment.
2. Read Nehemiah 1–2 and familiarize yourself with the story of how Nehemiah rebuilt the wall of Jerusalem.
3. Secure permission to use a junior or senior high school campus. Be sure to find out if there are restricted areas where students are not permitted to walk. Predetermine where students will gather before and after the vision walk.
4. Photocopy the handout.

Teaching Outline

Opening

PRAY—Gather students together on the school campus and open with prayer. Pray that God would help students see their school campus the way he sees it. Ask God to give students clarity about how they can make a difference in the spiritual condition of their schools.

TEACH—We are here to learn how God wants to use each of us on our school campuses. Although this may not be your school, while we're here it will represent the school you attend. It's not an accident or a coincidence that you attend the school you do. God has a plan for each of you to make a spiritual difference at your schools. We are going to learn more about how to make a spiritual difference by looking at the life of Nehemiah.

Nehemiah was an Old Testament prophet and a young leader used by God to do great things. God used Nehemiah to rebuild the wall of Jerusalem after it had been destroyed. Nehemiah knew he needed to assess the damage to the wall before he could repair it. In order to make his assessment, he took a walk to examine the wall for himself.

ACTION—Ask a student to read Nehemiah 2:11–13: "Three days after my arrival at Jerusalem, I slipped out during the night, taking only a few others with me. I had not told anyone about the plans God had put in my heart for Jerusalem. . . . I went out through the Valley Gate, past the Jackal's Well, and over to the Dung Gate to inspect the broken walls and burned gates."

TEACH—What Nehemiah did that night was to take a vision walk. He walked around to see what God wanted him to see and to find out how God wanted to use him to rebuild the wall. We are here to take our own vision walks and to assess the spiritual condition of our schools. Just as Nehemiah had to closely examine the damage to the wall of Jerusalem before he could repair it, we need to look closely at the damage that has been done to the spiritual condition of our schools. Then we will have a better idea how to ask God to use us to repair the damage. As you take your vision walk, your challenge is to make three bold prayer requests.

ACTION—Distribute the pens and handouts.

Prayer Request 1: God, help me to see my school the way you see it.

TEACH—The first bold prayer request is God, help me to see my school the way you see it. By praying this prayer you are asking God to show you how your school needs to be rebuilt spiritually and what your part should be in making it happen. God may see that your school needs prayer and knowledge of his truth. God may lead you to start a prayer meeting or Bible study on campus. God may see your school as a spiritual harvest where students are ready to hear the good news of his grace and love. Or God may lead you to share your faith and motivate other Christians to share their faith on campus. These are just a few examples of what God may show you when you look at your school the way he does. As you pray during your vision walk, ask God to help you see how you can help to rebuild your campus spiritually.

Prayer Request 2: God, give me opportunities to share my story with one of my non-Christian friends.

TEACH—The second bold prayer request is God, give me opportunities to share my story with one of my non-Christian friends. Listen to what Nehemiah did.

ACTION—Ask a student to read Nehemiah 2:18: "Then I told them about how the gracious hand of God had been on me, and about my conversation with the king. They replied at once, 'Good! Let's rebuild the wall!' So they began the good work."

TEACH—Just as Nehemiah shared with his friends what God had done in his life, we need to tell our friends the story of how God has changed our lives. That's why it's important to ask God to give you opportunities to share your story with one of your seeking friends. Nehemiah's friends were so motivated by his story, they immediately signed up to rebuild the wall of Jerusalem. When your non-Christian friends hear how a personal relationship with Christ has changed your life, there's a good chance they'll be motivated to learn more about Christianity. As you take your vision walk, ask God to bring to mind the name of a friend he wants you to share your story with. Write that friend's name on your handout. We will pray for all of our friends later when we come back from our vision walks.

Prayer Request 3: God, give me success in helping my friends become Christians and give me the approval of those in authority at my school.

TEACH—The third bold prayer request is God, give me success in helping my friends become Christians and give me the approval of those in authority at my school. Listen to the prayer Nehemiah prayed before asking the king for approval to rebuild the wall of Jerusalem.

ACTION—Ask a student to read Nehemiah 1:11: "'O Lord, please hear my prayer! Listen to the prayers of those of us who delight in honoring you. Please grant me success now as I go to ask the king for a great favor. Put it into his heart to be kind to me.'"

TEACH—We can follow Nehemiah's example by asking God to give us success with two things. First, by helping our friends come to know Christ. Pray that God would give you opportunities to have intentional conversations about spiritual matters. Ask God to soften your friend's heart and make it open to coming to church with you. Remember, this is a spiritual battle and we need to constantly ask God to help us share Christ with our friends.

Second, we need to ask God to give us favor with those in authority at our schools. People in authority at our schools include teachers, coaches, and the principal. Ask God to soften their hearts so they would consider sponsoring a Christian club on campus or maybe even be in prayer as you share Christ with other students at school. Having favor with those in authority would definitely be an advantage in changing our campuses for God.

Now it's time to take our vision walks.

ACTION—Give students the following instructions:
- Walk around the school alone and in complete silence. This is a time to make yourself wholly available to God.
- Use the three prayer requests on the handout to guide your thoughts and prayers.
- Here are three examples of how to use your walk as a way to pray for your school.

    1. Imagine a normal day at your school. Walk around the buildings or on the athletic fields and think about words that are spoken and activities that happen. Think about what you have seen and heard on your school campus that would be displeasing to God. As you pray, ask God to show you how you can make a difference in rebuilding the spiritual condition at your school.

2. Think about the different students you walk by every day. Look around and imagine students hanging out in different groups. Ask God to bring to mind a friend you need to share your story with.

3. Think of your teachers as you walk by classrooms. Imagine what it would be like to have favor with them as you rebuild the spiritual condition of your campus.

• Ask God what he wants you to see and hear as you walk. Write down any insights or leadings from God on your handout.

• You'll have fifteen minutes and then we'll meet back here.

Inform students if there are any restricted areas on campus where they are not permitted to walk. Pray for students before releasing them for their vision walks. After fifteen minutes, gather the group back together.

TEACH—We're going to take some time in small groups to share what we've just experienced on our vision walks.

ACTION—Ask students to gather in groups of three or four and give them ten minutes to share the most significant experience or insight from their vision walk.

After ten minutes, call the group back together.

Closing

TEACH—We're going to close by taking some time to pray for the friends whose names we wrote down on our handouts. We'll go around the group one at a time and say our friends' names out loud. Then we'll pray and ask God to use each of us to help our friends become Christ-followers.

ACTION—Go around the group and have students say out loud the name of the friend they wrote on their handout.

PRAY—Thank God for the names he placed on the hearts of the students. Ask him to give them opportunities and courage to tell their friends about God's love.

TEACH—This is a significant moment in our student ministry and in the lives of many people on our school campuses. God can use each one of you to rebuild the spiritual walls of your schools!

At the bottom of your handout is a place for you to write the name of your school. Go ahead and fill that in now. Written above it is Nehemiah 2:17: "'Let us rebuild the wall.'" Rebuilding the spiritual walls of your school starts today. It starts by seeing a vision and praying boldly. Pray that God will allow us to see our schools the way he wants us to see them. Pray that God will give us opportunities to share our stories and see our friends come to know Christ. Pray that God would give us favor with those in authority over us. What has happened today is the start of rebuilding the spiritual walls of the junior high and high school campuses around our community. God can use each of you to make an eternal difference at your schools this year.

PRAY—God, give us the eyes to see what you see. And give us the faith to believe that you will answer our prayers. Thank you for this time, and we thank you in advance for all that you are going to do!

VISION MOMENT 14

ONE LIFE AT A TIME

Purpose

To challenge every student to share Christ with one friend during the school year.

Overview

This vision moment takes place indoors. Students gather in a room other than their regular meeting room. They write the name of a non-Christian friend on an index card. The cards are collected, taken into the regular meeting room, and taped to every other chair. Students enter their regular meeting room and sit in a chair without an index card. They are challenged to imagine every empty chair filled by the end of the school year with the people whose names are written on the cards.

To help a friend make the decision to accept Jesus as forgiver and leader, students need to commit to a three-step strategy:

Step 1: Pray for your friend with boldness and confidence. We need to believe God can make a difference in our friends' lives (Matt. 21:22).

Step 2: Tell your friend the story of how God changed your life. Our stories are important, and our friends want to hear what we have to say (John 9:25).

Step 3: Invite your friend to church to see and hear what being a Christ-follower is all about. This is a great way to introduce friends to other Christians and help them learn more about Christianity (Acts 2:42–43).

Materials

- Bibles
- Index cards—one for every student
- Pens/pencils—one for every student
- Masking tape
- Chairs—twice as many as the expected number of students
- Photocopies of the "One Life at a Time" handout, page 142

Preparation

1. Read through the entire moment, familiarizing yourself with the teaching points and action steps before leading your group through the moment.
2. Select a room other than your regular meeting room in which to start.
3. Set up your regular meeting room with twice as many chairs as the number of students expected to attend.
4. Ask an adult volunteer to distribute index cards to students as they arrive, collect the cards after students have written on them, and tape the cards to every other chair in the regular meeting room while you continue teaching.
5. Photocopy the handout.
6. Consider planning a special outreach event designed specifically for non-Christians. At the end of this lesson, let students know when the event will take place so they can act on what they've learned by inviting their non-Christian friends.

Teaching Outline

Opening

ACTION—Have a volunteer at the door to distribute pens/pencils and index cards to students as they enter the first room.

PRAY—Gather students together and open in prayer. Ask God to help students see how he wants to use them this year to lead their friends into a personal relationship with Jesus.

TEACH—Jesus calls us to be light in a dark world. He wants us to share the good news about his love, grace, and forgiveness with our non-Christian friends. In this lesson we will learn how to do this. You will be challenged to make a commitment to take three strategic steps to help lead one friend into a personal relationship with Jesus this year.

Step 1: Pray for your friend with boldness and confidence.

TEACH—The first step we need to commit to is pray for your friend with boldness and confidence.

ACTION—Ask a student to read Matthew 21:22: "'If you believe, you will receive whatever you ask for in prayer.'"

TEACH—This verse says we need to come to God believing he will grant our prayer requests. This means having faith and confidence that God wants to make a difference in our friends' lives. We need to ask God to give us opportunities to share what God has done in our lives and to explain to our friends how God can make a difference in their lives too. We're going to act on this step right now by naming one friend and making a commitment to pray with boldness and confidence that this friend will become a Christian this year.

ACTION—Instruct students to write the name of one friend on their index cards. When students are finished writing, ask the volunteer to collect the cards. The volunteer should take the cards to the regular meeting room and tape one card to every other chair. The cards should be taped face out so the names are visible. The volunteer will have about ten minutes to do this before the group enters the room.

TEACH—We have just identified a friend we want to pray for this year. Our commitment is to pray that they would experience God's love and become Christians. This commitment starts right now. Remember the promise of Matthew 21:22: "'If you believe, you will receive whatever you ask for in prayer.'" We need to come before

God with confidence and boldness, believing he will make a difference in our friends' lives. We're going to take a moment right now to
pray for our friends.

ACTION—Give students the following instructions:
- Partner with one other person.
- Pray first for the friend whose name you wrote down; then
  pray for each other. Ask God to give your prayer partner
  perseverance to keep praying for his or her friend with boldness and confidence.

After five minutes, call the group back together.

Step 2: Tell your friend the story of how God changed your life.

TEACH—The second step we need to commit to is tell your
friends the story of how God changed your life. As Christians, we
have unique stories to tell of how we met God and received his amazing gift of forgiveness and grace. Your story is so important there are
at least three reasons you need to tell it to your friends. The first reason is that your friends are interested. Real friends want to know
about each other's lives; they want to understand each other's
thoughts, priorities, and experiences.

The second reason your story is important is that your friends
will relate to it. Chances are, you and your friends have similar interests and backgrounds. Most of the time, your friends will be able to
relate to your story, whether you've been a Christian all your life or
you've just been a Christian for a short time. Your friends will relate
to your story because they can relate to you.

The third reason your story is important is that it's hard to argue
with. When friends hear how God has changed your life, it's hard for
them to deny the reality of what you've experienced and that what
you believe in is true. It is up to us to look for opportunities to share
our stories, believing God will answer our prayers and use our stories in powerful ways.

There's a passage in the Bible that shows how powerful a personal story can be. When Jesus healed a blind man, the religious
rulers at that time weren't happy about it. They called in the man

Jesus healed and tried to get him to say bad things about Jesus. Listen to what the man said in response.

ACTION—Ask a student to read John 9:25: "'I don't know whether he is a sinner,' the man replied. 'But I know this: I was blind, and now I can see!'"

TEACH—The blind man didn't have all the answers, but he did have a story to tell about what God had done in his life: "I was blind, and now I can see!" There wasn't anything the religious rulers could say to deny the truth of the man's story. And that's how it is with our stories of coming to Christ—we simply need to be ready to tell the story of what God has done, and is continuing to do, in our lives.

This second step of the three-step strategy also starts now. In the first step we prayed for our friends; now we need to tell our stories. Since our friends aren't here, we're going to practice telling our stories to each other.

ACTION—Give students the following instructions:
- Partner with one other person.
- Each of you will have three minutes to tell your story to your partner.
- Your story of coming to Christ should include three parts:
     1. BC—your life Before Christ
     2. MC—your experience of Meeting Christ
     3. AC—how your life is different After Christ

Give students an example of how to share their stories by briefly sharing your own story—Before Christ, Meeting Christ, After Christ.

Alert students when three minutes are up so the other partner can begin telling his or her story.

After a total of six minutes, call the group back together.

TEACH—Isn't it exciting to hear how God has changed our lives? I hope you've been encouraged by hearing each other talk about what God has done. Your stories will encourage your non-Christian friends as well.

Step 3: Invite your friend to church to see and hear what being a Christ-follower is all about.

TEACH—The third step we need to commit to is invite your friend to church to see and hear what being a Christ-follower is all about. When our friends come to church with us, it's a great opportunity for them to meet our Christian friends, hear truth from God's Word, and begin learning what the Christian life is all about. It's also a time to get their questions answered and to change the misconceptions they may have about being a Christ-follower. We're going to take a few minutes right now to come up with some of the topics your seeking friends may be interested in hearing about.

> **ACTION**—Give students the following instructions:
> *   Partner with one other person.
> *   Share the name of the friend you would like to invite to church.
> *   Think of two or three issues or questions your non-Christian friends have about God or Christianity.
> *   Write these down on your handout.
> *   Pray together, asking God to soften your friends' hearts and make them willing to come to church with you.
> After about five minutes, call the group back together.

TEACH—What issues or questions do you think your non-Christian friends would like to hear about? We'll try to address some of these in future gatherings so you can invite your friends.

> **ACTION**—Take a few minutes to listen to and write down students' responses.
> Ask a student to read Acts 2:42–43: "They joined with the other believers and devoted themselves to the apostles' teaching and fellowship, sharing in the Lord's Supper and in prayer. A deep sense of awe came over them all, and the apostles performed many miraculous signs and wonders."

TEACH—These verses from Acts 2 describe the excitement the first Christians felt as they gathered together and prayed. They built community with each other and really believed God could change lives. That's what we are doing today—we are believing and trusting God by praying for our friends, by telling our stories, and by committing to invite our friends to church. We believe God is going to change lives and continue to add to our numbers the friends we love and care about.

To catch the vision of what God can do in our ministry this year if we keep our commitment to follow these three steps, please follow me into the next room.

ACTION—Ask students to follow you into the room where the index cards are taped to every other chair. Instruct them to sit in a chair without a card taped to it. Begin teaching after all students are seated.

Closing

TEACH—Look around the room. On the chair next to you is the name of someone's friend—a friend who matters to God, a friend someone has committed to pray for, tell their story to, and invite to church. Imagine how exciting it would be at the end of the year if the chair next to you had an actual person in it instead of just a card with a name on it. What if all of these chairs were filled with the friends who have made decisions to know and follow Christ? Wouldn't that be exciting! And think about what would happen to our youth ministry—it would double in size! What's so exciting about this is not just the numbers—it's the changed lives these names represent. This vision can happen. Each of you can make a difference—one life at a time—if you commit to this three-step strategy:

Step 1: Pray for your friend with boldness and confidence.

Step 2: Look for opportunities to tell your friends the story of how God changed your life.

Step 3: Invite your friend to church to see and hear what being a Christ-follower is all about.

If you are willing to make this commitment for the coming year, I really believe God can change the life of each person represented by the card on the chair next to you. But it's up to you. If you are willing to take these steps with the friend God has placed on your heart, I invite you to stand right now as a sign of your commitment.

ACTION—Ask students to stand and then lead them in prayer. Invite students to pray out loud, one at a time, asking God to use them to make a difference in the lives of their friends. After three or four students have prayed, close with your own prayer.

PRAY—Ask God to help students pray for their friends with boldness and confidence. Pray students will have the courage to share their stories and to invite their friends to church. Thank God in advance for all he is about to do, believing the people represented by the names on the chairs will become Christians this year.

Part 5

Service
Impacting the World

Overview

In the Great Commission (Matt. 28:16–20), Jesus told his disciples to "go and make disciples of all the nations." God cares about and is concerned for every person in every country—and he asks us to care too. He calls us to make an eternal impact every day in our world. The vision moments in this section are designed to open the eyes and soften the hearts of students to see beyond their needs to the needs of others, motivating them to be difference-makers in their world through serving.

15. Making an Impact
Purpose: To remind students that one young life committed to God can make a Kingdom impact on the world.
Scripture: 1 Samuel 17:14–17; 1 Samuel 17:38–40; 1 Samuel 17:26, 45–46; 1 Samuel 17:50

16. Dream Big for God
Purpose: To encourage and challenge students to be difference-makers in the world for God.
Scripture: Psalm 27:14; Jeremiah 29:11; Matthew 28:19; 1 Timothy 4:12

17. Brighter Lights
Purpose: To challenge students to let their spiritual light shine for others and to impact the world around them.
Scripture: Isaiah 58:10; Matthew 5:14–16; Matthew 28:20; John 8:12; John 15:5; Acts 13:47; Galatians 5:22–23; Ephesians 4:29; Philippians 2:14

Assessment

Directions

Use this assessment to evaluate students' needs for teaching and training about the importance of serving others. For each statement, place an X on the continuum closest to the response that best describes your students. Marks on the left side of the continuum indicate students would benefit from a vision moment in that area.

My students . . .   **Making an Impact**
(Go to page 111.)

Don't think they can make any Kingdom impact	Feel they may have some impact on others but are not sure	Believe they can make a difference but aren't sure how	Are committed to allowing God to use them to make a difference	Consistently experience God using them to make a kingdom impact

My students . . .   **Dream Big for God**
(Go to page 117.)

Have little or no desire to follow God's plans for their lives	Would like to be difference-makers but think they are too young or inexperienced	Feel torn between following God's plans and their own plans	Consistently pray for and pursue what God wants them to do	Are confident God uses them and actively seek to make a difference in their world

My students . . .   **Brighter Lights**
(Go to page 124.)

Have little or no connection with God	Are sometimes connected with God, allowing him to work within them	Have a connection to God and are starting to allow God to work through them to reach others	Allow God to use them consistently and strategically to make an impact	Consistently go beyond the point they would naturally and comfortably extend themselves to meet the needs of others

MAKING AN IMPACT

Purpose

To remind students that one young life committed to God can make a Kingdom impact on the world.

Overview

This vision moment takes place at a lake or pond. Students learn about three character qualities found in young King David's life—reliability, confidence, and loyalty—and how God used David to slay Goliath because of these qualities. Students learn they can slay giants in their own lives when they develop these same qualities. After a time of reflection and prayer, students throw a stone into the water to symbolize victory over their giant. The resulting ripples across the water symbolize the "ripples" students could make in the world for God by developing these three qualities in their lives.

Every student can make an impact on this world for God by developing the three character qualities evidenced in the life of young King David.

Character Quality 1: Reliability. David stayed faithful in the small things (1 Sam. 17:14–17).

Character Quality 2: Confidence. David accepted who he was and who he was in the process of becoming (1 Sam. 17:38–40).

Character Quality 3: Loyalty. David was not afraid to take a stand for God (1 Sam. 17:26, 45–46).

Materials

- Bibles
- Stones—one for every student

Preparation

1. Read through the entire moment, familiarizing yourself with the teaching points and action steps before leading your group through the moment.
2. At least a week ahead, find a suitable location at a nearby lake or pond. Secure any necessary permission needed to use this location.

Teaching Outline

Opening

PRAY—Gather the group together and open in prayer. Ask God to teach each student how developing strong character qualities at a young age can allow God to use them to make an eternal impact on the world.

TEACH—God wants each of us to be difference-makers in his kingdom. But how do we become the difference-makers he wants us to be? What do we need to do, or what qualities do we need to have in our lives that will allow us to be ready to be used effectively by God? We are going to take a look at the life of young King David and how the qualities he possessed allowed God to use him to make an impact in his kingdom.

Character Quality 1: Reliability

TEACH—The first character quality of David's we want to examine is reliability. Listen to this passage about David.

ACTION—Ask a student to read 1 Samuel 17:14–17: "David was the youngest of Jesse's sons. Since David's three oldest brothers were in the army, they stayed with Saul's forces all the time. But David went back and forth between working for Saul and helping his father with the sheep in Bethlehem. For forty days, twice a day, morning and evening, the Philistine giant strutted in front of the Israelite army. One day Jesse said to David, 'Take this half-bushel of roasted grain and these ten loaves of bread to your brothers.'"

TEACH—David was told to tend sheep while his older brothers went off to fight a war with the Philistines. At one point his father asked him to take food to his brothers in battle and report back on how they were doing. Because he was the youngest, David's role was basically to be the delivery boy. He wasn't seen as someone who could join in the battle and make a difference. How do you think David might have felt about everyone thinking he was too young to make a contribution?

ACTION—Allow a few students to respond before proceeding. Possible responses:
- He felt sad that he could not help in the fight.
- He felt that people didn't understand his strong faith and desire to serve God.
- He felt angry that they saw him as just a kid and not a young man who could make a difference.

TEACH—David was probably frustrated at times, but there's no record that he complained. Instead, he was reliable and did his job. David was responsible with what he was asked to do. God had a much bigger plan for David, but David first had to take care of small responsibilities before God could use him for greater things. David had to demonstrate he could be trusted.

Character Quality 2: Confidence

TEACH—The second character quality we see in David is confidence—he had confidence in who God made him. This confidence came through the day King Saul finally agreed to allow David to face Goliath. Here's what happened.

ACTION—Ask a student to read 1 Samuel 17:38–40: "Then Saul gave David his own armor—a bronze helmet and a coat of mail. David put it on, strapped the sword over it, and took a step or two to see what it was like, for he had never worn such things before. 'I can't go in these,' he protested. 'I'm not used to them.' So he took them off again. He picked up five smooth stones from a stream and put them in his shepherd's bag. Then, armed only with his shepherd's staff and sling, he started across to fight Goliath."

TEACH—Saul tried to make David into someone he wasn't, by putting David in heavy armor he wasn't used to. David had been a shepherd who fought off wild animals with stones and a slingshot, not with a helmet and sword. Saul meant well, but his armor wasn't what David needed to defeat the giant. David was confident that the same tools God gave him as a shepherd to defeat lions and bears could also defeat Goliath. David did not try to become someone he was not. Instead, he remained confident in who God had made him.

This is still true for us today. God wants to use you just the way you are—you do not have to become something or someone you are not. You just need to have confidence to be who God made you to be.

Character Quality 3: Loyalty

TEACH—The third character quality we see in young David is loyalty. David was not afraid to take a stand for God. Listen to David's response to his fellow soldiers and then to Goliath.

ACTION—Ask a student to read 1 Samuel 17:26 and 45–46: "David talked to some others standing there to verify the report. 'What will a man get for killing this Philistine and putting an end to his abuse of Israel?' he asked them. 'Who is this pagan Philistine anyway, that he is allowed to defy the armies of the living God?' . . . David shouted in reply, 'You come to me with sword, spear, and javelin, but I come to you in the name of the LORD Almighty—the God of the armies of Israel, whom you have defied. Today the LORD will conquer you, and I will kill you and cut off your head. And then I will give the dead bodies of your men to the birds and wild animals, and the whole world will know that there is a God in Israel!'"

Distribute the stones.

TEACH—We all know how the story ends.

ACTION—Ask a student to read 1 Samuel 17:50: "So David triumphed over the Philistine giant with only a stone and sling."

TEACH—David killed Goliath with a single stone. God gave David exactly what he needed to defeat the giant. All David needed to do was believe God was in control and that he would not let David be defeated. David remained loyal and stood by God without losing faith, no matter how difficult the circumstances were.

This is also true today. God is faithful and able to defeat the giants in our lives just as he helped David defeat Goliath. As we develop David's three character qualities—reliability, confidence, and loyalty—God will use us to slay giants. Giants are anything that threaten our spiritual health and growth. These include things like temptations, prejudice, or even those internal voices that deceive you into thinking you're not smart enough, strong enough, or talented enough to realize your dreams. Today, God is still in control and looking to help young giant-slayers like you fight the giants you face in your everyday life.

ACTION—Have students walk over to the edge of the water.

TEACH—In just a moment, we're going to throw our stones into the water. When you throw your stone, pay attention to how the ripples from one stone eventually spread across the whole lake. It's a great picture of the impact one person can have and how one person can be used to make an eternal difference in God's kingdom.

Before throwing your stone in the water, take a couple of minutes to dream big for God. Think about the giants in your life that need to be slain. Remember, God is faithful and will help you to defeat your giant. Also, think about what you want to do for God. Dream big and allow God to give you a clear picture of how he wants to use you. Spend some time in prayer to give your giant to God. Ask him for his power to be released within you so you can defeat it with his help.

When you finish praying, throw your stone into the water. Let it be a symbol of victory over your giant and how God will be glorified in this victory. Watch the stone hit the water and the ripples it makes. These symbolize how God wants to use you to have a rippling effect in the world around you and make eternal difference for his kingdom.

ACTION—Allow students a few moments to reflect and pray. After five to seven minutes (when every student has thrown his or her stone into the water), call the group back together.

Closing

PRAY—Pray that God would enable each student to be a giant-slayer for him. Ask God to help students stay reliable, confident, and loyal to what he has called them to do so they can make their own ripples in this world for his glory.

VISION MOMENT 16

DREAM BIG FOR GOD

Purpose

To encourage and challenge students to be difference-makers in the world for God.

Overview

This vision moment takes place indoors. Students are challenged to commit to being difference-makers for God by stepping into a circle that represents the world. They receive a personal passport containing a commissioning letter from God along with the name of a country to pray for.

Each student can be a difference-maker in the world by following three instructions from God's Word.

Instruction 1: Don't let anyone look down on you because you are young. We can have confidence in who God made us to be (1 Tim. 4:12).

Instruction 2: Wait for the Lord. Be patient and wait for God to give clarity (Ps. 27:14).

Instruction 3: Go and make disciples of all nations. We need to be willing to go where God calls us (Matt. 28:19).

Materials

- Bibles
- Photocopies of the "Dream Big for God" letter (personalized for each student), page 143
- Envelopes—one for every student
- Index cards—one for every student

- Duct tape or masking tape
- Large map of the world

Preparation

1. Read through the entire moment, familiarizing yourself with the teaching points and action steps before leading your group through the moment.

2. Using the "Dream Big for God" letter (page 143) as a template, write a personalized letter to each student. If possible, handwrite the letters. Otherwise, type the letters and personalize them by putting the name of each student at the beginning and in the text of the letter.

3. Put each letter in an envelope. The envelope should look as official and professional as possible and be personally addressed to each student. Write or stamp the word *passport* on the outside of the envelope.

4. Write the name of a different country on every index card. Place one card in each envelope. Seal the envelopes.

    Option: You can help students pray more specifically for the country on their index card by adding a few facts about the country or by naming specific needs to pray for. Visit Web sites for Christian mission organizations, such as World Vision, for specific ideas on how to pray for those in needy countries.

5. Using duct tape, make a circle on the floor large enough for all students to stand inside it at the same time.

6. Lay the map of the world on the floor in the center of the circle.

7. Place the sealed envelopes around the edge of the map, making sure students' names can be read.

Teaching Outline

Opening

PRAY—Gather students together and ask them to sit around the outside of the circle. Open with prayer. Ask God to give students a clear vision of what he wants them to do for his kingdom work.

TEACH—We are going to learn how we can become the difference-makers God wants us to be in this world.

ACTION—Ask a student to read Jeremiah 29:11: "'For I know the plans I have for you,' says the LORD. 'They are plans for good and not for disaster, to give you a future and a hope.'"

TEACH—This is true for each of you—God has good plans for your life! He has an amazing plan for every one of us to do great things for his kingdom. The question we need to ask and answer is "How do we find out God's plans for our lives?" We can begin to answer this question by following three instructions from God's Word.

Instruction 1: Don't let anyone look down on you because you are young.

TEACH—The first instruction is don't let anyone look down on you because you are young. This comes straight from one of the Bible's greatest heroes, the apostle Paul.

ACTION—Ask a student to read 1 Timothy 4:12: "Don't let anyone think less of you because you are young. Be an example to all believers in what you teach, in the way you live, in your love, your faith, and your purity."

TEACH—Why do you think the apostle Paul told his young disciple, Timothy, not to let anyone look down on him because he was young?

ACTION—Allow several students to respond before proceeding. Possible responses:
- He knew that older people might try to discourage him because they didn't think he was old enough to be trusted with responsibilities.
- Paul wanted to encourage Timothy and let him know he could be used mightily by God.

- Paul wanted to remind Timothy that God looks at the heart of a person, not at how old they are.

TEACH—Paul knew people would try to discourage young Timothy from thinking he could do great things for God—to dismiss him just because of his age. Paul told Timothy not to be discouraged by this; instead, he encouraged Timothy to be an example to older believers by how he spoke, how he loved others, by his strong faith, and by his commitment to purity. In other words, Paul told Timothy, "Don't hold back because you are young! Lean into the fact that God wants to use you to make a difference."

Paul's words are also true for you. God wants to make a difference in your life. You can't let others discourage you from what God wants to do with your life. Make the decision now not to let anyone look down on you because you are young. Instead, set an example of how a young believer can make a difference for God.

Instruction 2: Wait for the Lord.

TEACH—The second instruction to follow to help you learn God's plan for your life is wait for the Lord. Listen to this verse from the Psalms.

ACTION—Ask a student to read Psalm 27:14: "Wait patiently for the LORD. Be brave and courageous. Yes, wait patiently for the LORD."

Although God has plans for our lives, there may be times when it won't be clear what he wants us to do. At these times we need to wait for God to give us clarity. We need to be patient. In his own time, God will give us a clear understanding of his will. But don't confuse patience with passivity or laziness. The key to knowing God's plans for our lives is to faithfully continue to ask him to reveal them to us.

So be patient but pray continually. On a regular basis, ask God questions such as: "What do you want for my life?" "What are you calling me to do in the church?" "Where do you want me to get involved?" Then wait and watch. God will answer. He promises he will.

Instruction 3: Go and make disciples of all the nations.

TEACH—The third instruction for learning God's will is go and make disciples of all the nations. This is what Jesus charged his disciples to do just before he ascended into heaven.

ACTION—Ask a student to read Matthew 28:19: "'Therefore, go and make disciples of all the nations, baptizing them in the name of the Father and the Son and the Holy Spirit.'"

TEACH—The key word here is "go"! To make an impact in the world, we need to be willing to go where God calls us. Remember, God has the best plans for us—he's not going to call us into a life where we'll feel trapped and unfulfilled. Life with God should be an exciting adventure. He wants the best for us. He loves us. But God needs to know we're willing to say yes to wherever he wants to send us.

The question you need to answer is "Am I willing to go wherever God calls me?" The only way to find God's will for your life is to be willing to trust him completely. We're going to take a few minutes to pray on our own about our responses to the three instructions we've been talking about. As you pray, tell God whether or not you're willing to say yes to all three instructions:

1. Will you refuse to let anyone look down on you because you are young?
2. Will you wait patiently for God to reveal his plans?
3. Will you go wherever God calls you?

If you are willing to say yes to God on all three of these points, pray this simple prayer: "God, my answer is yes—my life is yours." I'm going to give you a few minutes to make that decision and to pray.

ACTION—Allow students three to five minutes to pray silently, then call the group back together.

TEACH—In just a moment you'll have an opportunity to publicly acknowledge the decision you've just made. If you said yes to God, you'll step across the tape line in front of you as a sign of your willingness to go anywhere in the world God calls you.

On the ground around the map are passports with your names on them. If you choose to step over the line, pick up the passport with your name on it and hold it until I tell you to open it.

PRAY—Ask God to give each student the strength and courage to dream big for him.

TEACH—If you're willing to make this decision—to say yes to God with your whole life—step across the line as a sign of your commitment to go anywhere in the world God calls you. Then pick up your passport.

ACTION—Allow enough time for students to make their decisions and pick up their envelopes.

Closing

TEACH—I'm very excited for each of you who made the decision to say yes to God. In a moment, you'll step outside the circle, find a place to sit down, and open your passport. Read the instructions God is giving you. As you read your letter, be encouraged that God wants you to dream big for him—that he has a vision and plans for your future. In your passport you'll also find a card with the name of a country written on it. For the next seven days, you are to pray that God would reign in that country. As you think about and pray for your country, let that country represent your willingness to go anywhere in the world God may call you.

ACTION—Instruct students to step out of the circle and find a quiet place nearby to open their passports and to pray. After three to five minutes, call the group back together and have students sit inside the circle.

TEACH—I hope you were encouraged by the letter you received from Jesus. It's important that we take very seriously the commitments we've made. Pray for your country for the next seven days, letting God know each night that you are open to go wherever he calls you.

Before we close, let's go around the group and share the names of the countries we'll be praying for.

ACTION—Have each person say out loud the name of the country he or she will be praying for.

PRAY—Ask God to reveal to each student his vision and plans for their lives. Pray that God would use their prayers to make a difference around the world.

VISION MOMENT 17

BRIGHTER LIGHTS

Purpose

To challenge students to let their spiritual light shine for others and to impact the world around them.

Overview

This vision moment takes place indoors. Using a small table lamp as a symbol of spiritual light, students are taught to let their light shine in the world. They write four checklist items on light bulbs and take the bulbs home as a reminder to let their spiritual light shine to others.

We can be spiritual light to others and impact our world by following a maximum impact checklist.

Checklist Item 1: Plug in. Apart from Christ we can do nothing (John 8:12; John 15:5).

Checklist Item 2: Turn on. We need to decide to let our light shine to others (Gal. 5:22–23).

Checklist Item 3: Set out. Be a light to those around us 24-7 (Matt. 5:14–16).

Checklist Item 4: Extend beyond. Think, dream, and go beyond the point we would typically extend ourselves (Acts 13:47; Matt. 28:20).

Materials

- Bibles
- Photocopies of the "Brighter Lights" handout, page 144
- Table lamp

- Small table
- Twenty-five-foot extension cord
- Light bulbs—one for every student
- Medium-size cardboard box
- Fine-tip permanent markers—one for every student

Preparation

1. Read through the entire moment, familiarizing yourself with the teaching points and the action steps before leading your group through the moment.
2. Set the lamp on the table and position the table so students will be able to sit around it. The lamp should be unplugged.
3. Have an extension cord plugged in and nearby, ready to be used during the moment.
4. Put light bulbs in the cardboard box and have them nearby, ready to distribute.
5. Photocopy the handout.

Teaching Outline

Opening

PRAY—Gather students together around the table and open with prayer. Ask God to give students a clear picture of how they can shine brightly for him. Ask him to help them understand what it means to let their light shine to the farthest corners of their world.

ACTION—Distribute the handouts.

TEACH—We need to be ready to effectively reach out to the world around us, with our spiritual light shining as brightly as possible. Our spiritual light is simply our efforts to allow Christ to work in us and through us to reach out to others. Listen to Matthew 5:14–16: "'You are the light of the world—like a city on a mountain, glowing in the night for all to see. Don't hide your light under a basket! Instead, put it on a stand and let it shine for all. In the same way, let your good deeds shine out for all to see, so that everyone will praise your heavenly Father.'" We have to make sure that we shine as brightly as possible. So, just as a pilot runs through a preflight checklist to make sure everything is working well before takeoff, we are going to run through a maximum impact checklist to make sure each one of us is working well before we try to make an impact on the world. We want to shine brightly so others will be attracted to our spiritual light and come to know Christ as a result.

Checklist Item 1: Plug in.

ACTION—Distribute the light bulbs and fine-tip permanent markers.

TEACH—The first item on our maximum impact checklist is plug in.

ACTION—Ask students to write the words *Plug In* on their bulbs. (Point out that they will be writing several phrases on the light bulb so they will leave enough room to write.)

As you teach on Checklist Item 1, use the lamp cord to demonstrate the need to plug into a power source. Start with the lamp unplugged and then plug it in at the appropriate time in the teaching.

TEACH—We can have the most powerful light strategically placed for maximum effect, but if it's not plugged in—connected to the power source—nothing will happen when we turn the switch. In the same manner, before we can be a light to others in this dark world, we need to be connected to our power source—Jesus. In John 8:12 Jesus said, "I am the light of the world. If you follow me, you won't be stumbling through the darkness, because you will have the light that leads to life." For our light to shine consistently and brightly, we need to be plugged in at all times. Being plugged in means building our relationship with God by reading the Bible, spending time in prayer, and practicing other spiritual disciplines. In John 15:5 Jesus said, "Those who remain in me, and I in them, will produce much fruit. For apart from me you can do nothing." Without this connection to Christ we will not be able to do anything for him. Before we go any further, we need to assess our connection to God. We'll do this in small groups.

ACTION—Instruct students to gather in groups of three and discuss the following questions from the handout:
- Where do you feel you are right now with God? Are you plugged in? Unplugged? Somewhere in between?
- What, if anything, is holding you back from being completely plugged into God?

After seven to ten minutes, call the group back together.

Checklist Item 2: Turn on.

TEACH—Now that we've covered the first item on the maximum impact checklist—plug in—it's time to move onto the second item: Turn on.

ACTION—Ask students to write the words *Turn On* on their light bulb.

As you teach on Checklist Item 2, use the lamp to demonstrate the need to be turned on in order for the bulb to light up and shine. Start with the lamp turned off and then turn it on at the appropriate time in the teaching.

TEACH—A lamp produces no light until someone decides to turn it on. Turning on our spiritual light means to not only allow God to work in us, but also through us to impact people around us. Listen to the Bible's description of what it means to let our spiritual light shine: "But when the Holy Spirit controls our lives, he will produce this kind of fruit in us: love, joy, peace, patience, kindness, goodness, faithfulness, gentleness, and self-control" (Gal. 5:22–23a). These are the characteristics others will see shining out from us when we live lives that are plugged into God and turned on to the Holy Spirit. As we go about our daily lives, everything we do will either attract people to us or turn them away from us. The decision to turn on our light is one we need to make every day. It is how we will attract others to the Light—by letting God work in us and then through us. This is how we let our spiritual light shine out to everyone we encounter. Let's take a moment to hear what the Bible says about what it really means to let our light shine.

ACTION—Ask four different students to read the following verses out loud from the handout:

- "Feed the hungry and help those in trouble. Then your light will shine out from the darkness, and the darkness around you will be as bright as day" (Isa. 58:10).
- "But when the Holy Spirit controls our lives, he will produce this kind of fruit in us: love, joy, peace, patience, kindness, goodness, faithfulness, gentleness, and self-control" (Gal. 5:22–23).
- "In everything you do, stay away from complaining and arguing" (Phil. 2:14).
- "Don't use foul or abusive language. Let everything you say be good and helpful, so that your words will be an encouragement to those who hear them" (Eph. 4:29).

Instruct students to gather again in groups of three and use these verses as a reference point as they discuss the following question from the handout: In what area of your life is it difficult to let your light shine?

After about five minutes, call the group back together. Invite students to share their responses with the group. Allow three or four students to share before proceeding.

Checklist Item 3: Set out.

TEACH—On our maximum impact checklist we're up to item three: Set out.

ACTION—Ask students to write the words *Set Out* on their light bulbs.

As you teach on Checklist Item 3, demonstrate the need to have the lamp set out in order for its light to shine and light up the room. Contrast the difference between a lamp hidden under the table and a lamp set on top of the table. Start by placing the lamp on the floor under the table. Place the lamp back on the table at the appropriate point in the teaching. The lamp should remain lit throughout.

TEACH—In Matthew 5:15 Jesus said, "Don't hide your light under a basket! Instead, put it on a stand and let it shine for all." A lamp is made to provide light. We are made to provide light too. The world needs to see our light shining. We shine when we encourage fellow believers and illuminate the path to Christ for those who don't yet know him. We cannot allow ourselves to be content with letting our light shine only at church, on Sundays, when we are with a certain group of friends, or when it's convenient. We need to be brave and let our light shine for Jesus wherever we are, whoever we're with, and whatever situation we might be in. Being set out means being a 24-7 (twenty-four-seven) light to those around us—a light that shines twenty-four hours a day, seven days a week.

ACTION—Ask students the following questions from the handout:
- In practical terms, what does it mean for you to be "set out"?
- Do you ever hide your light? Why?

Ask the questions one at a time, allowing several students to respond to each one before proceeding.

Checklist Item 4: Extend beyond.

TEACH—We've finally reached the end of our maximum impact checklist. The final item is: Extend beyond.

ACTION—Ask students to write the words *Extend Beyond* on their light bulbs.

As you teach on Checklist Item 4, demonstrate the ability of the extension cord to move the lamp to places it could not go when using only its own cord. Start with the lamp on the table, plugged directly into the wall and turned on. At the appropriate time in the teaching, unplug the lamp from the wall socket and plug it into the live extension cord. As you teach about extension, move the lamp around, demonstrating how the extension cord enables the lamp to shine in places it couldn't go without the extension cord. The lamp should be lit throughout.

TEACH—God often wants us to think, dream, and go beyond what we would typically do for him because when we extend ourselves, it brings us to a place of complete dependence on him. On its own, the lamp has a limited range. With an extension cord we can take the lamp places it couldn't go with just its regular cord. When we talk about extending beyond to impact the world, we mean pushing beyond what we are used to and comfortable with. We extend ourselves to a point of vulnerability—a place where we might feel awkward or unsure of ourselves. Extending ourselves means going beyond our comfort zones in ministry. This might mean traveling somewhere to serve others, reaching out to a neighbor, or serving someone we have never met. This does not mean that we put ourselves in an unsafe or dangerous position. But it does mean that we should extend beyond where we are comfortable and stretch ourselves into circumstances that are more difficult for us. Whatever it is, it will be something so big that God's power will be very evident because we couldn't do it on our own.

ACTION—Ask a student to read Acts 13:47: "'I have made you a light unto the Gentiles, to bring salvation to the farthest corners of the earth.'"

TEACH—In this verse God asks us to extend our light to the farthest corners of the world. He wants us to extend ourselves beyond our natural limits, knowing that we can rely on his promise in Matthew 28:20: "'And be sure of this: I am with you always, even to the end of the age.'" We're going to take some time to talk about this with a partner.

ACTION—Give students the following instructions:
- Partner with one other person and discuss the following question from the handout: If you faced no barriers, no fears, no limitations, what would your dream be for extending your light for God?
- Write a few words on your light bulb that capture your extension dream, for example, an event, a person's name, a phrase, or an important day or time.

After seven to ten minutes, call the group back together and have students sit in a circle. Invite them to share their dreams with the group. Allow several students to respond before proceeding.

TEACH—It is great to dream big for God and to go after those dreams. It's important to remember that one life changed for eternity is an amazing thing. Whatever your dream, whatever the farthest corner of the world is for you, remember that God will meet you there—you just have to extend yourself and show up.

Closing

ACTION—Ask students to write "Matthew 5:14" on their light bulbs as you read the verse to them: "'You are the light of the world—like a city on a mountain, glowing in the night for all to see'" (Matt. 5:14).

TEACH—This verse is addressed to each one of you. You are to be the light that makes a maximum impact on your world. Stay plugged into Jesus. Make that daily choice to turn your light on and set yourselves out for everyone to see. Extend beyond your comfort zones and dream big for God.

ACTION—Give students the following instructions:
- Place your light bulbs in the center of the circle so everyone can see them.
- Take a moment to think about all the dreams these light bulbs represent.
- Imagine what it would look like to see these dreams become reality.

After a moment of silence, call the group back together and ask students to get back with their partners to pray about their dreams of how God could use them to be a light to their world.

Instruct students to retrieve their light bulbs.

TEACH—Your light bulb is a symbol of your commitment to be ready for God to use you, extend you, and shine through you. Take it home and put it in a prominent place where you will see it often and be reminded of what God wants for you.

PRAY—Ask God to help the students continue to dream big and extend themselves to serve others and make an impact in their world. Pray that students would let their spiritual light shine bright to those around them and extend beyond their comfort zones to make an impact in the world for him.

A Moldable Heart

Vital Question 1:
What is the condition of my heart right now?

Directions: Take a moment to reflect on the condition of your heart. How open are you to God's will for your life and your relationships? Place an X on the line below to indicate whether your heart is closer to being soft and responsive to God or closer to being hard and unresponsive to God.

Soft and — Hard and
Responsive   Unresponsive

Vital Question 2:
Who is molding my heart?

Directions: Take a moment to reflect on who is molding your heart. Are you influenced more by God's values or the world's values? Place an X on the line below to indicate which has the stronger influence on your life and relationships.

God — World

Discussion Questions
- What things have the ability to draw your heart away from God?
- Proverbs 2:1–5 says, "My child, listen to me and treasure my instructions. Tune your ears to wisdom, and concentrate on understanding. Cry out for insight and understanding. Search for them as you would for lost money or hidden treasure. Then you will understand what it means to fear the LORD, and you will gain knowledge of God." Considering this verse, what actions can you take to keep your heart soft and responsive to God?

A Replenished Heart

Fact 1: Jesus is the only one who can satisfy the needs of our hearts.

"'If you believe in me, come and drink! For the Scriptures declare that rivers of living water will flow out from within'" (John 7:38).

"'But the water I give them takes away thirst altogether. It becomes a perpetual spring within them, giving them eternal life'" (John 4:14).

Discussion Questions
- What does Jesus have the ability to do for empty lives?
- What does he ask us to do in order to drink in his living water?

Fact 2: God is able to fill our hearts with purpose and satisfy our needs.

"They are like trees planted along the riverbank, bearing fruit each season without fail. Their leaves never wither, and in all they do, they prosper" (Ps. 1:3).

"The LORD will guide you continually, watering your life when you are dry and keeping you healthy, too. You will be like a well-watered garden, like an ever-flowing spring" (Isa. 58:11).

Discussion Questions
- What are some of the things the world tells you will fill your life (for example, a lot of money, sex, success)?
- What have you seen to be the result when people try to fill their lives with the world's answers instead of God's truth? Explain.
- According to Psalm 1:3 and Isaiah 58:11, what are the results of a life filled by God?

Fact 3: God expects his followers to serve one another.

"'But among you it should be quite different. Whoever wants to be a leader among you must be your servant, and whoever wants to be first must become your slave. For even I, the Son of Man, came here not to be served but to serve others, and to give my life as a ransom for many'" (Matt. 20:26–28).

Whom can I serve this week with God's love?

_____

(Write in the name of the person you will serve this week.)

How might I serve this person? (List two or three specific ideas.)

134

Who You Are

Who you are . . .

- You are a child of God (John 1:12).
- You are the salt of the earth (Matt. 5:13).
- You are the light of the world (Matt. 5:14).
- You are Christ's friend (John 15:15).
- You are free from the power of sin in Christ (Rom. 6:6–7).
- You are God's child and you will share his treasures—for everything God gives to his Son, Christ, is yours too (Rom. 8:17).
- You are the temple of God and the Spirit of God lives in you (1 Cor. 3:16).
- You are joined to the Lord and you are one spirit with him (1 Cor. 6:17).
- You are a member of Christ's body and a necessary part of it (1 Cor. 12:27).
- You are a new person (2 Cor. 5:17).
- You are a child of God through faith in Christ Jesus (Gal. 3:26).
- You are God's masterpiece. He has created you anew in Christ Jesus (Eph. 2:10).
- You are a member of God's family (Eph. 2:19).
- You are created in God's likeness—righteous, holy, and true (Eph. 4:24).
- You are chosen by God—holy and dearly loved (Col. 3:12).
- You are a child of light and of the day; you do not belong to darkness and night (1 Thess. 5:5).

Say the Words

Truth 1: Words are powerful.

"But encourage one another daily, as long as it is called Today, so that none of you may be hardened by sin's deceitfulness" (Heb. 3:13 NIV).

Discussion Questions
- Share a time when you were encouraged at the right time with the right words from a Christian friend.
- Why was your friend's encouragement meaningful to you? How did it make you feel?

Truth 2: Two are better than one.

"Two people can accomplish more than twice as much as one; they get a better return for their labor. If one person falls, the other can reach out and help. But people who are alone when they fall are in real trouble. And on a cold night, two under the same blanket can gain warmth from each other. But how can one be warm alone? A person standing alone can be attacked and defeated, but two can stand back-to-back and conquer. Three are even better, for a triple-braided cord is not easily broken" (Eccles. 4:9–12).

Discussion Questions
- Share a time when someone was there for you when you were in need.
- How did it make you feel?
- How did it change your attitude or situation?

Truth 3: Iron sharpens iron.

"As iron sharpens iron, a friend sharpens a friend" (Prov. 27:17).

Discussion Questions
- Share a time when you received correction—words of truth—from a friend. How open were you to the correction? How did you feel afterward? What difference did it make in your life?
- Share a time when you corrected a friend with words of truth. Was it difficult for you? Why or why not? How did the person respond?

A 2:14 Attitude

"Your attitude should be the same that Christ Jesus had" (Phil. 2:5).

"Though he was God, he did not demand and cling to his rights as God. He made himself nothing; he took the humble position of a slave and appeared in human form. And in human form he obediently humbled himself even further by dying a criminal's death on a cross" (Phil. 2:6–8).

Quality 1: Christ was a servant.

"Don't think only about your own affairs, but be interested in others, too, and what they are doing" (Phil. 2:4).

Servant Attitude

I serve only myself	I serve if I have to	I serve others sometimes	I love to serve others whenever I can

Quality 2: Christ was humble.

"He made himself nothing; he took the humble position of a slave and appeared in human form" (Phil. 2:7).

Humble Attitude

I am a prideful person	I look out only for me	I try to see others' interests over my own	I want to have a humble attitude

Quality 3: Christ was obedient.

"And in human form he obediently humbled himself even further by dying a criminal's death on a cross" (Phil. 2:8).

Obedient Attitude

It is very difficult for me to submit to authority	It is easy for me to submit to authority

Between the Lines Football Field Diagram

```
                  XXXXXXXXXXXXXX
- - - - - - - - - - - - - - - - - - - End Zone - - - - - - - - - - - - - - - - - - -


      XXX   Students line up behind hurdle 1 or 2   XXX
- - - - - - /Hurdle 1/ - - - - - - - 10-Yard Line - - - - - - /Hurdle 2/ - - - - - -

      Students then walk to here, after knocking down hurdles.
- - - - - - - - - - - - - - - - - - - 20-Yard Line - - - - - - - - - - - - - - - - - -


      XXX   Students line up behind hurdle 3 or 4   XXX
- - - - - - /Hurdle 3/ - - - - - - - 30-Yard Line - - - - - - /Hurdle 4/ - - - - - -

      Students then walk to here, after knocking down hurdles.
- - - - - - - - - - - - - - - - - - - 40-Yard Line - - - - - - - - - - - - - - - - - -


      XXX   Students line up behind hurdle 5 or 6   XXX
- - - - - - /Hurdle 5/ - - - - - - - 50-Yard Line - - - - - - /Hurdle 6/ - - - - - -

   Students walk to here, after knocking down hurdles, and line up.
                  XXXXXXXXXXXXXX
- - - - - - - - - - - - - - - - - - - 40-Yard Line - - - - - - - - - - - - - - - - - -

   Students continue walking until they reach the 20-yard line.
- - - - - - - - - - - - - - - - - - - 30-Yard Line- - - - - - - - - - - - - - - - - -

   At 20-yard line, students grab hands and walk into End Zone.
- - - - - - - - - - - - - - - - - - - 20-Yard Line - - - - - - - - - - - - - - - - - -


- - - - - - - - - - - - - - - - - - - 10-Yard Line- - - - - - - - - - - - - - - - - -


- - - - - - - - - - - - - - - - - - - End Zone - - - - - - - - - - - - - - - - - - -
```

Finish—Hang school banners between these goal posts.
Students should gather here for prayer at the end of the vision moment.

X = **Students**. Students begin on the **sideline**, then line up along the goal line in the end zone.

/**Hurdle #**/. Place hurdles at the hash marks—these lines should already be marked on all fields.

You Matter

Review this list of strengths and abilities. Circle any that describe talents and gifts you think you might have.

- I am good at organizing people, tasks, and/or events.
- I enjoy using my artistic skills (art, drama, music, photography, etc.).
- I am a good judge of a person's character.
- I enjoy speaking in front of people.
- I enjoy encouraging people.
- I openly tell people about my faith.
- I pray with confidence, trusting God to answer my prayers.
- I like to help wherever needed.
- I enjoy leading others, and others tend to follow me.
- I enjoy meeting new people and helping them feel welcome.
- I am good at resolving conflicts.
- I help others to perform to the best of their capabilities.
- I enjoy doing things for people who are in need.
- I am good at caring for a small group of people.
- I am a good listener and can relate well to others.
- I know the Word of God well and can use Scripture to help others.
- I am good at standing up for what is right and challenging others to do so.

I believe my top two strengths are:

Strength 1:

Strength 2:

Write your top two strengths on the back of your puzzle piece and then complete the sentence below by listing two or three ways you can contribute to our ministry. After completing the sentence, write it on the back of your puzzle piece.

I can use my strengths in our ministry by . . .

Called to Contribute

Truth 1:
Physical death is certain.

"You are a mist that appears for a little while and then vanishes" (James 4:14 NIV).

Truth 2:
Eternal life is available to everyone.

"For if you confess with your mouth that Jesus is Lord and believe in your heart that God raised him from the dead, you will be saved" (Rom. 10:9).

"'I am the resurrection and the life. Those who believe in me, even though they die like everyone else, will live again'" (John 11:25).

Truth 3:
God asks us to be involved
in bringing people to him.

"But how can they call on him to save unless they believe in him? And how can they believe in him if they have never heard about him? And how can they hear about him unless somebody tells them? And how will anyone go and tell them without being sent? That is what the Scriptures mean when they say, 'How beautiful are the feet of those who bring good news!'" (Rom. 10:14–15).

"'Therefore, go and make disciples of all the nations, baptizing them in the name of the Father and the Son and the Holy Spirit. Teach these new disciples to obey all the commands I have given you. And be sure of this: I am with you always, even to the end of the age'" (Matt. 28:19–20).

Discussion Questions
- What would it mean for you to take an active role in telling your friends about Christ?
- What is holding you back from telling your friends about Christ?
- What first step can you take to share Christ with your friends?

Vision Walk

Prayer Request 1:
God, help me to see my school
the way you see it.

"Three days after my arrival at Jerusalem, I slipped out during the night, taking only a few others with me. I had not told anyone about the plans God had put in my heart for Jerusalem. . . . I went out through the Valley Gate, past the Jackal's Well, and over to the Dung Gate to inspect the broken walls and burned gates" (Neh. 2:11–13).

Prayer Request 2:
God, give me opportunities to share my story
with one of my non-Christian friends.

"Then I told them about how the gracious hand of God had been on me, and about my conversation with the king. They replied at once, 'Good! Let's rebuild the wall!' So they began the good work" (Neh. 2:18).

_____

My Friend's Name

Prayer Request 3:
God, give me success in helping my friends
become Christians and give me the approval of
those in authority at my school.

"'O Lord, please hear my prayer! Listen to the prayers of those of us who delight in honoring you. Please grant me success now as I go to ask the king for a great favor. Put it into his heart to be kind to me'" (Neh. 1:11).

"'Let us rebuild the wall . . .'"—Nehemiah 2:17

_____

My School's Name

One Life at a Time

Step 1:
Pray for your friend with
boldness and confidence.

- Partner with one other person.
- Pray for the friend whose name you wrote down.
- Pray for each other. Ask God to give your prayer partner perseverance to keep praying for his or her friend with boldness and confidence.

Step 2:
Tell your friend the story of how
God changed your life.

- Partner with one other person.
- Tell your story to your partner.
- Your story of coming to Christ should include three parts:
  1. BC—your life Before Christ
  2. MC—your experience of Meeting Christ
  3. AC—how your life is different After Christ

Step 3:
Invite your friend to church to see and hear
what being a Christ-follower is all about.

- Partner with one other person.
- Share the name of the friend that you would like to invite to church.
- Write down two or three questions or topics you believe your non-Christian friends would be interested in hearing about.
  1.
  2.
  3.
- Close in prayer, asking God to soften the heart of your friend to come to church with you.

Dream Big for God

Dear (insert student's name),

You are fearfully and wonderfully made. I have loved you with an everlasting love. I have gifted you, equipped you, and given you a counselor—the Holy Spirit—to guide you and to lead you every day of your life. I have a plan for your life that will enable you to prosper—a plan to give you a future and a hope.

You are a chosen person. I called you out of darkness into a wonderful life with me. Once you were not my child, but now you are a child of mine. Once you had not received mercy, but now you have received mercy.

All authority in heaven and on earth has been given to me, therefore, (insert student's name), go and make disciples of all nations, baptizing them in the name of the Father and the Son and the Holy Spirit and teaching them to obey everything I have commanded you. And, surely, I am with you always to the very end of the age.

I love you, my child. Dream big for me.

Jesus

Brighter Lights

Checklist Item 1: Plug in.

"'I am the light of the world. If you follow me, you won't be stumbling through the darkness, because you will have the light that leads to life'" (John 8:12).

"'Those who remain in me, and I in them, will produce much fruit. For apart from me you can do nothing'" (John15:5).

Discussion Questions

- Where do you feel you are right now with God—completely plugged in, unplugged, or somewhere in between?
- What, if anything, is holding you back from being completely plugged into God?

Checklist Item 2: Turn on.

"Feed the hungry and help those in trouble. Then your light will shine out from the darkness, and the darkness around you will be as bright as day" (Isa. 58:10).

"But when the Holy Spirit controls our lives, he will produce this kind of fruit in us: love, joy, peace, patience, kindness, goodness, faithfulness, gentleness and self-control" (Gal. 5:22–23).

"In everything you do, stay away from complaining and arguing" (Phil. 2:14).

"Don't use foul or abusive language. Let everything you say be good and helpful, so that your words will be an encouragement to those who hear them" (Eph. 4:29).

Discussion Question

- In what area of your life is it difficult to let your light shine?

Checklist Item 3: Set out.

"'Don't hide your light under a basket! Instead, put it on a stand and let it shine for all'" (Matt. 5:15).

Discussion Questions

- In practical terms, what does it mean for you to be "set out"?
- Do you ever hide your light? Why?

Checklist Item 4: Extend beyond.

"'I have made you a light unto the Gentiles, to bring salvation to the farthest corners of the earth'" (Acts 13:47).

"'And be sure of this: I am with you always, even to the end of the age'" (Matt. 28:20).

Discussion Question

- If you faced no barriers, no fears, and no limitations, what would your dream be for extending your light for God?

SCRIPTURE INDEX

<u>Scripture</u>	<u>Vision Moment</u>
Matthew 14:23	2. A Moldable Heart
Matthew 14:25–33	2. A Moldable Heart
Matthew 14:29	9. Between the Lines
Matthew 14:30–31	9. Between the Lines
Matthew 20:26–28	4. A Replenished Heart
Matthew 21:22	14. One Life at a Time
Matthew 22:36–40	12. Called to Contribute
Matthew 25:14–30	10. You Matter
Matthew 25:21	9. Between the Lines
Matthew 28:19	16. Dream Big for God
Matthew 28:19–20	12. Called to Contribute
Matthew 28:20	17. Brighter Lights
Mark 12:30	6. Reflections
John 4:14	4. A Replenished Heart
John 7:38	4. A Replenished Heart
John 8:12	17. Brighter Lights
John 9:25	14. One Life at a Time
John 11:25	12. Called to Contribute
John 15:5	17. Brighter Lights
Acts 2:42–43	14. One Life at a Time
Acts 13:47	17. Brighter Lights
Romans 1:12	5. Who You Are
	6. Reflections
Romans 10:9	12. Called to Contribute
Romans 10:14–15	12. Called to Contribute
Romans 12:2	1. A Submissive Heart
	5. Who You Are
Romans 14:19	6. Reflections
1 Corinthians 9:19	11. The Race
1 Corinthians 9:24	11. The Race
1 Corinthians 9:25–26	11. The Race
1 Corinthians 9:27	11. The Race
1 Corinthians 12:20, 25	9. Between the Lines
1 Corinthians 12:21–26	10. You Matter
Galatians 5:22–23	6. Reflections
	17. Brighter Lights
Ephesians 4:29	17. Brighter Lights
Philippians 1:6	5. Who You Are

Scripture	Vision Moment
Philippians 2:4	8. A 2:14 Attitude
Philippians 2:5	8. A 2:14 Attitude
Philippians 2:6–8	8. A 2:14 Attitude
Philippians 2:7	8. A 2:14 Attitude
Philippians 2:8	8. A 2:14 Attitude
Philippians 2:14	8. A 2:14 Attitude
	17. Brighter Lights
Philippians 3:14	11. The Race
Philippians 4:13	9. Between the Lines
Colossians 3:5–10	3. A Renewed Heart
1 Thessalonians 5:11	5. Who You Are
	6. Reflections
1 Timothy 4:12	16. Dream Big for God
Hebrews 3:13	7. Say the Words
Hebrews 8:12	3. A Renewed Heart
Hebrews 12:1–3	9. Between the Lines
James 4:14	12. Called to Contribute
James 5:16	3. A Renewed Heart
1 John 1:9	3. A Renewed Heart

Also Available

The TruthQuest™ Inductive Student Bible (NLT)
Black bonded leather with slide tab 1-55819-843-1
Blue bonded leather with slide tab 1-55819-849-0
Paperback with Expedition Bible Cover 1-55819-928-4
Hardcover 1-55819-855-5
Paperback 1-55819-848-2
Expedition Bible Cover only 1-55819-929-2

The TruthQuest™ Share Jesus without Fear
New Testament (HCSB) 1-58640-013-4

The TruthQuest™ Prayer Journal 0-8054-3777-0

The TruthQuest™ Devotional Journal 0-8054-3800-9

TruthQuest™ Books

Survival Guide: The Quest Begins!
by Steve Keels with Dan Vorm
0-8054-2485-7

Coming May 1, 2004
Survival Guide Spanish Edition
En Busca de la Verdad—
Plan de Accion
0-8054-3045-8

You Are Not Your Own:
Living Loud for God
by Jason Perry of Plus One
with Steve Keels
0-8054-2591-8

Living Loud: Defending Your Faith
by Norman Geisler & Joseph Holden
0-8054-2482-2

Getting Deep: Understand What You
Believe about God and Why
by Gregg R. Allison
0-8054-2554-3

Am I the One?: Clues to Becoming
and Finding a Person Worth
Marrying
by James R. Lucas
0-8054-2573-X

Something from Nothing:
Understand What You Believe
about Creation and Why
by Kurt Wise & Sheila Richardson
0-8054-2779-1

Commentaries
Coming July 1, 2004
Getting Deep in the Book of . . .
  Luke: Up Close with Jesus
  0-8054-2852-6
  Romans: A Life and Death Experience
  0-8054-2857-7
  James: Christian to the Core
  0-8054-2853-4
  Revelation: Never Say Die
  0-8054-2854-2
by Steve Keels
& Lawrence Kimbrough

Available at Your
Local Book Retailer

BROADMAN
&HOLMAN
PUBLISHERS

www.broadmanholman.com/truthquest